Traditional Gardens

Traditional Gardens

PLANS AND PLANTING DESIGNS

ROGER PLATTS

Photography Steven Wooster

CASSELL ILLUSTRATED

To my son, Thomas

First published in Great Britain in 2004 by Cassell Illustrated,
a division of Octopus Publishing Group Limited
2–4 Heron Quays, London E14 4JP

Distributed in the United States of America by
Sterling Publishing Co., Inc.,
387 Park Avenue South, New York, NY 10016-8810

A CIP catalogue record for this book is available from the British Library

ISBN 1 8440 3133 0

Editorial and Design: R & R Publishing
Pippa Rubinstein & Judith Robertson

Printed in China

CONTENTS

Climate zones
Suitable climate zones are included for the plants in this book. As a simple guide, the UK, lowland France and Germany, and the East and West Coast USA fall into zones 8 and 9 and all plants in this book should grow there. Northern USA, the Rockies, Canada and Eastern Europe are in zones 3–5.

INTRODUCTION

Where to start? When designing a garden, whether from scratch or working with an established garden, it is necessary to prioritize requirements. These are dictated usually by location, budget and practical considerations such as purpose: 'what is the garden to be used for?'

In presenting the information on each of the gardens in this book, I deal first with planning and how to approach the requirements for each garden. This is followed by the choice and positioning of structural elements that include paving, steps, walling, water features, pergolas and lawns. The choice of plants is then considered and a selection of some of the combinations and individual varieties pictured and described. The horticultural details here are necessarily brief and are designed to help the reader make their own selections. More information on any plant can always be obtained from a plant encyclopedia. The section on 'Getting the best from your garden' then looks at some of the techniques on how to deal with various soils, ground preparation and maintenance issues such as pruning and mulching.

When planning and, later, implementing the work on a garden, I normally start from the house or largest structure and work out. My advice when planning a traditional garden is always to keep the layout simple and do not let the design be driven by the need to include a specific feature. It is better to design a pleasing layout and then see how you can adapt it to include the required feature. The layout of pathways plays a large part in this as they naturally divide up the garden and create individual spaces that provide interest and potential for introducing special features.

Think about where you need height for shelter, screening or shade, or to soften a structure such as a corner of a garage, house or neighbour's wall. Make sure that you allow enough appropriate space for plants in these key areas to enable them to do the necessary screening, softening or shading. You will see throughout this book that in my designs, plants dominate the gardens. However, underneath the soft green living exterior is a strong supporting structure of stone, brick, timber, steel or concrete framework. The style, the shape and the proportions of paths, pergolas and seating areas must be carefully selected to provide the continuity and quality of construction that supports the planting. It is true that planting can cover up mistakes, unsightly materials or structures but poor design or construction normally shows through in the end and it is better to get the right structure in place from the start and only then rely on the plants to do their best for you.

When drawing the initial layout on paper it is essential at some stage to set it out on the ground and, to help the imagination, perhaps mark the position of trees and large shrubs using canes or stakes. I find the best method of marking out the layout shape is to use line

Above Use strong, simple structural features like this sturdy oak pergola to train climbing and rambling roses.

Right Create 'windows' in the planting. Here, a robinia tree and foxgloves frame the view of a pond in the distance.

paint, available in different colours in aerosol cans. Alternatives are sand, bamboo canes, hosepipes or rope. Whether it is a whole garden or simply an adjustment to the shape of a lawn and planted beds or an addition to a paved terrace, this is the best way to make a final decision on layout. When setting out the overall shape a number of practical considerations need to be addressed, such as position of manholes, underground services and existing trees. Consider the shortest route from, say, the back door of your house to the garage; a route that is made too circuitous is bound to be ignored by short-cutting across the lawn. Often a compromise to a design is required to fulfil both practical and visual requirements. Perhaps a stepped (zigzag) path or a curved path will get you from A to B just as easily but may look better than a straight one that slices the garden in two.

At the layout stage budget is not a major factor as it does not necessarily cost more to build a garden with a pleasing layout than it does to create one lacking balance and unity. The two elements that should not be compromised by budget are the layout of the garden and ground preparation.

My own appreciation of garden design started from the need to create appropriate areas to grow the wide range of plants that would look good together. However successful you may be with plant combinations and plant cultivation, if the supporting layout and structure are not in balance with the surroundings, the garden will never feel quite right.

Often a small adjustment to existing layouts can make huge improvements with relatively small cost. Look for these opportunities first, especially when making improvements to an existing garden. A good example is the shape of planted areas that often have a curve that is too shallow to have any impact. Indeed from a short distance away it may look like a straight line. To improve on this be bold with sweeping and exaggerated curves. This gives more depth and interest and sometimes even mystery to the garden. It may also provide more scope for planting and does not cost much to implement.

Left A rose-covered pergola underplanted with soft mauve and pink perennials gives a sense of richness and depth.

Right A pergola clad with *Rosa* 'Rambling Rector' provides shade over a seating area. *Cistus* x *purpureus* can be seen in the foreground.

The choice of materials for traditional gardens tends to be limited to natural materials such as stone, brick and timber. However, there are some good alternatives available, as can be seen with the paving for the first garden in this book. I try wherever it's possible to use local materials that are in keeping with the house and surrounding properties. Try to avoid using many different materials, which can result in making the garden over-fussy and do not create a sense of continuity. There may be a temptation to include gravel, timber, brick, stone, concrete, steel and more all in a small area, with the mistaken belief that you are creating lots of interest. The result is a mish-mash of materials that dominate the planting. Instead, it is important to keep the construction simple and allow the planting detail to dominate. The bolder the hard structure, buildings, paths and terraces. you have in place, the bolder the planting structure must be to balance this before the infill planting is introduced.

At this layout stage consideration of maintenance and seasonal interest must play a part and a proportion of evergreen plants included. As a rough guide I find that most traditional gardens have 20–30 per cent evergreen, which includes groundcover as well as structural planting. This will vary slightly depending upon the maintenance time available and the presence of existing plant structure.

The mix of deciduous and evergreen is important to ensure interest in a garden all year round. For example, an evergreen shrub such as box or myrtle can be surrounded with herbaceous plants that disappear in winter, leaving the evergreen to shine on its own. However, a deciduous shrub such as weigela or dogwood could be underplanted with evergreen groundcover, perhaps pachysandra or hellebores, to maintain interest during the bleak winter months. To maximize effect, perennial groundcover plants should always be used in drifts, rather than dotted about. This is mentioned in the various chapters and you will see how it is put to good effect in the accompanying photographs.

I hope this book will serve as a guide and inspiration for anyone to have the courage to go out and enjoy doing their garden and not be afraid to be bold with line paint, mushroom compost and secateurs!

Above A tapestry of foliage and perennial flowers.

Right Gentle colours and soft textured foliage and
flowers contrast with the paving and surround
the flowing water in this tranquil scene.

WINNING CHELSEA SHOW GARDEN

In existence for less than two weeks, this garden was viewed by more people over four days than the average garden in a lifetime – not surprising as it was the winning Show Garden at the 2002 Chelsea Flower Show. It was designed as an authentic sustainable garden and created to celebrate 75 years of the National Garden Scheme, with its promotion of 'open days' during which anyone can visit the participating private gardens for pleasure and inspiration. Carefully managed, this garden would give its owner a variety of aspects and planting to enjoy throughout the year, but particularly during the summer months.

PLANNING the GARDEN

The plan for this garden was devised to make the most of an area 16x14m (52½x46ft), mainly sunny and including a derelict area that has a charm of its own, merging into the long grass of a field skirting the walled garden.

In the contrived situation of a flower show there are, of course, some compromises that have to be made, such as allowing viewing by many thousands of visitors and taking account of the short build timescale (less than three weeks in this case). However, it is important to create a garden that is authentic and correct in all aspects, including layout, construction and planting. Some show gardens are more theatrical than others but all should follow a brief as if they were created for a client.

A technical brief was submitted to the Royal Horticultural Society before the show and used by them as the basis for judging the garden. It included a description of the theme, which is that of a walled garden, refurbished after years of dereliction with a view to opening for the National Garden Scheme several times throughout the summer months but also providing the owner with a place to take tea in the shade of the summerhouse or sit quietly by the sunny wall under the pergola in between open days.

This was not therefore simply an exercise to make the garden look attractive; it also had to fulfil the requirements set out in the brief. In this case the brief was prepared by the designer but in a real situation it would have been provided by the client or garden owner.

Various elements from the original walled garden of 75 years ago are used to provide features for a twenty-first century garden. The old galvanized trough utilized as a water feature with subtle lighting is matched with an old galvanized

The English shrub rose 'Chianti' underplanted with *Geranium sanguineum* and *Nepeta x faassenii*. Corner structure is created with the small but shapely Hebe 'Red Edge'.

corn bin with a lid and a cushion on top to create a seat, ideal to store your croquet set or gardening tools.

This is quite an intensively planted garden and, as with all things intensive, it requires high maintenance. However, it is full of interesting plants and most of the maintenance work involved is pruning to maintain the status quo rather than weeding and staking.

Created as part of a larger garden, the aspect is mainly sunny with a shady walk at the back and areas of shade created by the summerhouse and trees. Changes in level are linked by simple steps and there are perhaps more paths in proportion to the overall area than found normally, but these are necessary to give room for visitors to move around the garden and provide space and plenty of seating during 'Garden Open' days.

Walled gardens are normally, though not always, on level ground but this site was a bank rising up to 1.5m (5ft) from front to back. There was no doubt that in this case the garden had to be built on a single level due to the small space and therefore the whole site required digging out. The main function of the oak summerhouse is to provide shelter from sun, rain and wind and yet when sitting in it to give a sense of being part of the garden and surrounded by plants on all sides. Left open at the back, it was necessary to plant behind the building to provide a sense of depth and yet enclosure using a combination of shrubs and perennials.

The shady area behind the summerhouse created a space for woodland plants and a secluded spot to sit, hidden from the front. Indeed, a number of interviews were carried out during the show in this sheltered position tucked away from the crowds of visitors just a short distance away.

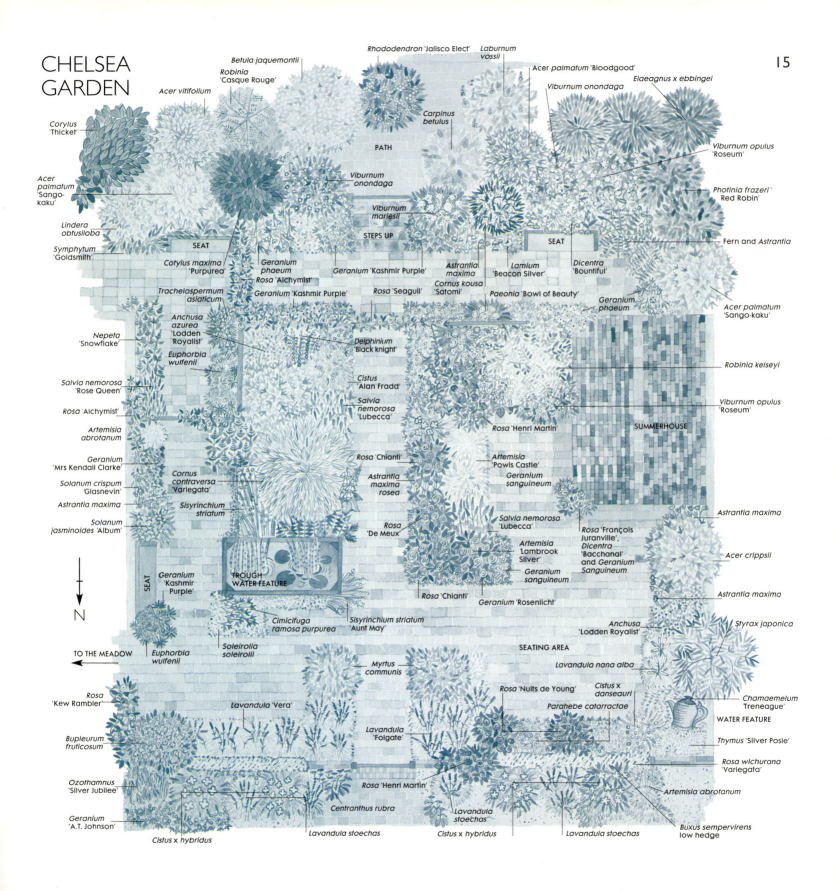

CHELSEA
GARDEN

Corylus 'Thicket'

Acer vitifolium

Betula jaquemontii

Robinia 'Casque Rouge'

Rhododendron 'Jalisco Elect'

Laburnum vossii

Acer palmatum 'Bloodgood'

Viburnum onondaga

Elaeagnus x ebbingei

Carpinus betulus

PATH

Viburnum opulus 'Roseum'

Acer palmatum 'Sango-kaku'

Viburnum onondaga

Photinia frazeri 'Red Robin'

Lindera obtusiloba

Viburnum mariesii

STEPS UP

SEAT

SEAT

Fern and Astrantia

Symphytum 'Goldsmith'

Cotylus maxima 'Purpurea'

Geranium phaeum

Rosa 'Alchymist'

Geranium 'Kashmir Purple'

Geranium 'Kashmir Purple'

Astrantia maxima

Lamium 'Beacon Silver'

Dicentra 'Bountiful'

Trachelospermum asiaticum

Cornus kousa 'Satomi'

Rosa 'Seagull'

Paeonia 'Bowl of Beauty'

Geranium phaeum

Acer palmatum 'Sango-kaku'

Anchusa azurea 'Lodden Royalist'

Nepeta 'Snowflake'

Euphorbia wulfenii

Delphinium 'Black knight'

Robinia kelseyi

Salvia nemorosa 'Rose Queen'

Cistus 'Alan Fradd'

Viburnum opulus 'Roseum'

Salvia nemorosa 'Lubecca'

Rosa 'Alchymist'

Rosa 'Henri Martin'

SUMMERHOUSE

Artemisia abrotanum

Rosa 'Chianti'

Artemisia 'Powis Castle'

Geranium 'Mrs Kendall Clarke'

Astrantia maxima rosea

Geranium sanguineum

Cornus contraversa 'Variegata'

Solanum crispum 'Glasnevin'

Astrantia maxima

Sisyrinchium striatum

Astrantia maxima

Salvia nemorosa 'Lubecca'

Solanum jasminoides 'Album'

Rosa 'De Meux'

Rosa 'François Juranville', Dicentra 'Bacchanal' and Geranium Sanguineum

Acer crippsii

Geranium 'Kashmir Purple'

SEAT

Artemisia Lambrook Silver'

Astrantia maxima

TROUGH WATER FEATURE

Geranium sanguineum

Rosa 'Chianti'

Geranium 'Rosenlicht'

N

Cimicifuga ramosa purpurea

Sisyrinchium striatum 'Aunt May'

Anchusa 'Lodden Royalist'

Styrax japonica

TO THE MEADOW

Euphorbia wulfenii

Soleirolia soleirolii

SEATING AREA

Lavandula nana alba

Chamaemelum Treneague'

Myrtus communis

Rosa 'Nuits de Young'

Cistus x danseauri

Rosa 'Kew Rambler'

Lavandula 'Vera'

Parahebe catarractae

WATER FEATURE

Bupleurum fruticosum

Lavandula 'Folgate'

Thymus 'Silver Posie'

Rosa wichurana 'Variegata'

Ozothamnus 'Silver Jubilee'

Artemisia abrotanum

Geranium 'A.T. Johnson'

Rosa 'Henri Martin'

Centranthus rubra

Lavandula stoechas

Buxus sempervirens low hedge

Cistus x hybridus

Lavandula stoechas

Cistus x hybridus

Lavandula stoechas

SPECIAL FEATURES

A blend of traditional old and new underlies the structure of this garden. The largest single feature is the tumbledown wall; in this case the whole structure was built on bare ground within several weeks. However, it represents a natural ruined wall that would be quite costly to reinstate. This shows how to leave it in a dilapidated state, provided it is safe, and clad with plants. The fact that it is partly tumbledown adds a certain charm.

Window and seat

Whether new or old, a window in a garden wall can provide a focal point and break up the line of what otherwise may be a boring expanse of brick. A famous example of this is at Sissinghurst Castle Gardens, where Vita Sackville-West constructed a metal criss-cross window in one of the many walls. Here I used the top of an old stable door. With an old oak frame and rusted metal bars, it fits well with the old brick wall and oak lintels across the adjacent door. Just below the window, but not directly in front, we positioned a seat that started life as a corn bin. Galvanized and heavily constructed it will last for years and has a useful lid and so can be used for storage. A thin waterproof cushion makes a good seat and the brick plinth enhances the appearance and sets the seat at a comfortable height. The position of the seat in relation to the window is important too. It should not sit directly underneath the window but should be set to one side of the line of the window.

Water feature

In keeping with the theme of reclaimed materials and galvanized features, a water tank that could have been a reservoir in an old greenhouse when the walled garden was in its heyday was modified to form a simple water feature. In fact it was probably a water header tank for a large building. Made of heavy duty steel and galvanized, I found this one at a farm sale. The older type and best galvanized tanks for water features, whether animal troughs or storage tanks, are those that are riveted rather than the

The sunny wall with an old oak and iron window is next to a doorway framed by an old beam. Roses scramble over the wall and *Erigeron karvinskianus* has seeded itself in cracks in the brickwork.

Right Delphinium flowers stand above a drift of rose, cistus and geranium, with 'Tumble' paving leading to stone steps and a simple wooden gate.

Below In the background, *Cornus controversa* 'Variegata' is underplanted with apricot foxgloves and *Eupatorium rugosum* 'Chocolate'. *Astilbe* 'Irrlicht' is to the right of the water tank and *Sisyrinchium striatum* 'Aunt May' is surrounded by *Geranium sanguineum* 'Album' in the foreground.

more modern seam-welded and pressed types. By housing this within a second tank sunk beneath the ground as a reservoir and with a circulating pump, a soothing, reflective water feature was created (see page 112 for details).

Paving

Getting the combination of old and new materials just right is often quite a challenge and because of the expense and shortage of old paving bricks I looked for modern alternatives. A range of paving blocks called 'Tumble' proved the answer and these provided the ideal link from a small area of old Victorian brick pavers at the front to the rugged Kentish ragstone steps at the back. To lay the paving, first an edge of pavers was set in concrete around the

perimeter and allowed to set. Sand was then spread in the middle and levelled to 1cm (½in) above the base of the cemented paving edge. This was then filled in with pavers gently tapped into position with a wooden block and, finally, a vibrating plate was passed over the pavers to force them into the sand bed, firming them down to the level of the cemented edge and tightly bonding them with sand forced up between each paver.

Green oak features

The front gate, pergola and summerhouse were all newly made for the garden from green oak timber that will, within a year or so, weather to an attractive silver-grey colour. The summerhouse and the pergola are connected and form a physical link from one corner of the garden to the other. This physical link visually holds the garden together and provides it with the unity required when mixing old with new. It also creates a variety of viewing angles that produce a sense of depth in a relatively small space. The summerhouse was roofed using reclaimed clay tiles fixed on oak battens to create an attractive feature both inside and out. The underside was illuminated at night by small spotlights shining across the roof timbers and battens, giving a soft and warm reflected light.

With a need for plenty of seating when the garden is open for the National Gardens Scheme, it was necessary to position chairs and benches in every possible corner without cluttering the space – especially as it is also a garden to be enjoyed by the owner for the rest of the year and should not look like a public park. Three old trestle benches with iron bases and wooden planks bolted on top were positioned discreetly without blocking pathways to blend into the planting and were

Rosa 'François Juranville' climbs up the summerhouse, at the base of which is a mix of perennials, *Geranium sanguineum, Sisyrinchium striatum* 'Aunt May' and *Dicentra* 'Bacchanal'.

A group of *Francoa sonchifolia* planted in Whichford pots surrounded by blue spires of *Salvia* 'Mainacht' and delphiniums. *Viburnum opulus* 'Sterile' and white aquilegias are growing in the background.

light enough to carry away for storage when necessary. Further seating is provided by a small round hardwood table and two chairs outside the summerhouse and a large hardwood table and set of chairs inside the summerhouse itself.

Teapot and teacup

A regular feature of the National Gardens Scheme gardens is the tea and cakes served to visitors and, to reflect this tradition, another water feature in the shape of a teapot and teacup was designed – a large terracotta teapot with a large spout and a hole in the base and a teacup with integral saucer also with a hole in the base. From a buried water tank with submersible pump, water is circulated through a pipe passing up through the hole in the base of the teapot and into the spout. The teapot is set at an angle for water to pour out of the spout and into the teacup below. The teacup has a rigid pipe glued and sealed through the hole in the bottom of the cup and positioned just below rim level to act as an overflow. This pipe passes down below the teacup and saucer into the water reservoir below. Once the flow has been adjusted it should be continuous and the reservoir simply requires topping up occasionally. Planting around this feature had to be carefully considered and chamomile was ideal to form a green carpet that could be surrounded by *Thymus* 'Silver Posie' and *Lavandula nana* 'Alba' to add a little height.

For that extra touch of authenticity, several teabags of English Breakfast tea in the reservoir provides the required colour – a gimmick, but it caught attention at the Flower Show.

The teapot and teacup water feature surrounded by a green carpet of chamomile with *Thymus* 'Silver Posie' and *Rosa wichurana* 'Variegata' tumbling over the wall. In the background are the rich blue flowers of *Anchusa azurea* 'Loddon Royalist'.

PLANTS and PLANTING

Planted close to the summerhouse and dominating the middle ground structural planting to the right of the main path is a *Robinia kelseyi* – a brittle tree that should be planted in sheltered places – which produces wonderful pea-like lilac-pink flowers during the early summer that look rather like pink laburnum. Because of its 'feathery' leaves, shade cast by this tree is light and underplanting of a wide range of varieties can be sustained. The robinia can be pruned but must be thinned not trimmed. Indeed, the more pruning this is given, the stronger the new growth tends to be. Another similar variety that will do the same job is *Robinia* 'Casque Rouge'. To screen off the back corner of the garden, *Viburnum opulus* 'Roseum' is planted underneath the robinia. This will require hard pruning immediately after flowering to keep it in check. It has attractive lime-green heads of flower in early summer that gradually turn creamy white. Under the viburnum, and in quite dry conditions because of the summerhouse roof overhang, are planted *Lamium* 'Pink Pewter' and *Geranium* 'Rosenlicht'. Further from the canopy, a drift of *Aquilegia* 'Norah Barlow' and *Aquilegia* 'The Bride' continue the pink-and-white theme with a cluster of deep pink *Dicentra* 'Bountiful' and *Geranium sanguineum* at the base of the summerhouse post. Climbing rose 'François Juranville' scrambles up the oak frame and *Rosa* 'Chianti' provides a splash of deep red at the corner of the bed.

Euphorbia characias spp. *wulfenii* underplanted with *Geranium* 'Kashmir Purple' makes a strong combination.

A centrepiece of *Cornus controversa* 'Variegata' underplanted with *Astilbe* 'Irrlicht' and *Digitalis* 'Sutton's Apricot'.

Euphorbia characias ssp. *wulfenii* (zones 6–10) bears lime-green bracts freely on tall fleshy green stems up to 1m (3ft) from mid-spring until early summer. The foliage is blue-green and an attractive architectural feature all year round. In ideal conditions (well-drained soil in full sun) this plant can be quite invasive, seeding freely, and may require thinning. For good results and a tidy plant, remove the stems as low as possible when the flowering heads become untidy, normally by early to midsummer (see page 137). This will allow new growth to thrive from the base on which next year's flowers will form and will retain fresh green stems throughout the year. Take care and wear gloves and long sleeves as the sap is poisonous and can cause skin rash and eye irritation.

Cornus controversa 'Variegata' (zones 5–8), the variegated giant dogwood, grows up to 8–10m (25–30ft) in height and width. Branches grow in striking horizontal layers and during late spring and early summer large flat heads of small creamy white flowers appear. It has new leaves of yellowish variegation that become white and green with pink tinges to the leaf margins as they age. This is a good tree to underplant as the colour scheme can go a number of ways – pink, white, cream, red, even pale yellow or apricot. The soil must be free draining but moisture retentive and fertile. For a smaller and more silvery alternative you could try *Cornus alternifolia* 'Argentea'.

Solanum crispum 'Glasnevin' scrambling up and over the wall with *Lindera obtusiloba* and *Acer palmatum* 'Sango-kaku' in the background.

Helichrysum rosmarinifolia 'Silver Jubilee' with a background of *Bupleurum fruticosum* and the upright habit of a highly scented *Rosa* 'Mrs John Laing'.

A dark blue *Delphinium* 'Black Knight' alongside *Digitalis* 'Sutton's Apricot'.

Solanum crispum **'Glasnevin'** (zones 9–11) is a vigorous climber that may require some hard pruning every spring. It is capable of attaining 5–6m (16–20ft) on a sunny wall or fence so requires plenty of room. The powder blue flowers with orange centres are good with any combination of yellow or cream such as *Rosa banksiae* 'Lutea' or *Rosa* 'Alchymist'. Flowering takes place during early summer with further intermittent flushes during late summer. As a member of the nightshade family, along with tomatoes and potatoes, the flowers resemble those of the tomato plant and it is commonly known as the potato vine. For success, grow in a sunny, sheltered position in rich well-drained but moisture-retentive soil.

Helichrysum rosmarinifolia **'Silver Jubilee'** (zones 8–10), also known as *Ozothamnus*, reaches 2m (6ft) high and 1m (3ft) wide. As the name suggests this plant has rosemary type foliage and it requires similar conditions, which are plenty of sun and good drainage. Rather susceptible to wind rock, especially in wet soils, it benefits from light pruning after flowering and harder pruning in late spring. Do not expect this plant to look good for more than five or six years, and less on heavier soils. It becomes rather woody over time but is still well worth growing for the striking silver foliage and soft pink flowers.

Delphinium **'Black Knight'** (zones 4–7) is one of the darkest purple delphiniums widely available and is versatile for a varied range of combinations. Delphiniums have a major predator: slugs. If you can overcome the slug problem then, with careful staking and regular watering, they will provide a long season of flowering. Choose good varieties such as 'Black Knight', 'Guinivere' or 'Astolat' of the Pacific hybrids range which grow to 1.2m (4ft). There are also many other good hybrids available. The stems of old-fashioned shrub roses provide good support for delphiniums as well as prolonging seasonal interest, so consider planting close to a canopy of shrub roses. They require full sun and well-drained, moist, very fertile soils.

Dark green shiny leaves provide a good foil for the fluffy scented white flowers of *Myrtus communis*.

Rosa 'Kew Rambler' smothers the wall and is covered in a mass of pale mauve-pink flowers.

Bright pink laburnum-like flowers of *Robinia kelseyi* hang from the light, feathery foliage.

Myrtus communis (zones 8–9) is the common myrtle and with its many attributes is a very useful plant. It is an evergreen shrub growing 2–2.4m (6–8ft) high and wide with shiny dark green aromatic leaves and scented fluffy white flowers during early to midsummer. If pruned hard every year, it forms a very bushy habit and can be used instead of box as structural planting in milder areas. Prune immediately after flowering in summer to encourage new growth that will ripen before winter and carry flowers the following summer. Alternatively, prune every two or three years in spring to allow the attractive black fruits to form after flowering; the fruits are held into late autumn. It requires a sheltered sunny position in well-drained soil.

Rosa 'Kew Rambler' (zones 5–9) is a very vigorous rose reaching over 6m (20ft), ideal to scramble over pergolas and through trees. It is a once-flowering variety, which means that for a period of about six weeks during early summer it is smothered with a mass of small pale pink single flowers with a white centre in large clusters. It has very thorny stems and the foliage is a rather bluish green, making it an attractive plant even before it flowers. By early autumn it will have large clusters of small red hips.

Robinia kelseyi (zones 5–10) is a small-growing variety of the false acacia tree that will reach 3–4m (10–15ft) high and wide. During early summer it is smothered with bright lilac-pink flowers that resemble laburnum in shape. Like laburnum, this tree is in the pea family and does not transplant very easily. The growth is very brittle and it should therefore be planted in a position sheltered from strong winds in fertile well-drained soil. Prune to keep a good shape by thinning out the longest branches rather than cutting them all back. Pruning tends to induce vigour and the aim with this tree is to maintain a light canopy and an attractive shape.

Rosa 'Alchymist' clambers over a pergola, the apricot-yellow flowers contrasting with the dark leaves of *Corylus maxima* 'Purpurea'.

Viburnum plicatum 'Mariesii' and *Digitalis purpurea* 'Excelsior Hybrids' underplanted with *Geranium clarkei* 'Kashmir Purple'.

Geranium x oxonianum 'Rosenlicht' smothers the base of *Artemisia absinthium* 'Lambrook Silver' with bright pink flowers that contrast with the silver foliage of the artemisia.

Rosa 'Alchymist' (zones 4–9) flowers only once and quite early in summer, so it is important to prune out old stems after flowering and tie in new growth as it appears throughout the summer. The flowers are profuse and sweetly scented. Give it plenty of room as it is very vigorous and thorny. It is a good variety to grow up into an old fruit tree or on a pergola and will grow up to a height of 4m (13ft). It is rather prone to mildew so is best grown on an open structure to encourage a free flow of air and in moisture-retentive soil.

Geranium clarkei 'Kashmir Purple' (zones 5–7) provides good groundcover and is best planted in drifts for good effect. The rich purple flowers associate well with dark green leaves and white flowers. It will often provide a second flush of flower if cut back severely after first flowering; otherwise, it can look rather untidy by midsummer. Plant in well-drained soil in sun or part shade. *Digitalis purpurea* 'Excelsior Hybrids' (zones 4–8) is a selected form of foxglove with flower colours from pink through mauves to white. They prefer moist but well-drained soil in sun or part shade. Do not skimp on the numbers you plant. For best effect plant close together with the odd plant dotted here and there as if self-seeded.

Geranium x *oxonianum* 'Rosenlicht' (zones 4–7) is excellent groundcover due to its easy cultivation and versatile nature. Best planted in drifts, it has a height and spread of 30–45cm (12–18in) and bright pink flowers continue all summer. Cut back hard after the first flush of flower to encourage new growth from the base and more flowers. It will tolerate part shade but thrives in full sun and any well-drained soil. *Artemisia absinthium* 'Lambrook Silver' (zones 4–9) grows 60–90cm (2–3ft) high with delicate silvery grey, feathery foliage. It tends to become straggly and is therefore best grown among other plants such as roses that can give it some natural support. The position it requires is very well drained and in full sun.

LANDSCAPED POND AND BOG GARDEN

Although part of a larger and older garden, this pond and bog area is still only a year old. Winding grass paths lead to gates in the fence surrounding the pond, which is clay lined and constructed to appear as near to a natural pond as is possible within a cultivated garden. Positioned in the lowest part of the garden, the planting springs up from the lush boggy margins, which are surrounded by a rustic fence. It is a small oasis designed to draw you from other parts of the garden and, once through the gate, to settle you into tranquil surroundings engulfed in planting.

PLANNING the GARDEN

Ponds in the landscape should look natural even though they are normally a contrived feature. In this case a natural style of pond was required to replace a formal Koi pool and the siting of it was dictated by existing contours and underground springs. The major feature of the design is the safety aspect as it required a fence to deter unaccompanied young children from approaching the water's edge.

This pond and bog garden is part of a much larger garden, so it was important that the scale was in keeping with the surroundings and the challenge was to avoid the whole pond looking completely isolated from the rest of the garden.

Most manmade ponds require a liner of some sort but we were fortunate here that underneath the thin stony soil there was heavy clay, which we dug out and used to puddle the sides. In this case a clay-lined pond was by far the best option because of a regular water supply and top-up from natural springs in the upper part of the garden. If a liner had been used, underground water pressure could have been

a problem, causing the liner to hippo – that is, balloon up inside the water. This can happen in areas that have a high water table, even with a good thick layer of soil on top of the liner. One must always remember to have an overflow to any pond in order to avoid flooding the rest of the garden.

It is always better to work with the surrounding and natural elements rather than against them, so a natural style of pond with a bog garden was the best choice in a position where a hole in the ground would fill up with water quite quickly.

Although this garden is in a suburban location, post-and-rail fencing was used so that it would blend with the rest of the garden and planting over time, becoming a less intrusive barrier. The setting was quite open with good views across fields and so a backdrop had to be created that would not block the views completely.

Grass paths wind through the wildflower area leading to a gate in the pond fence surround.

LANDSCAPED POND and BOG GARDEN

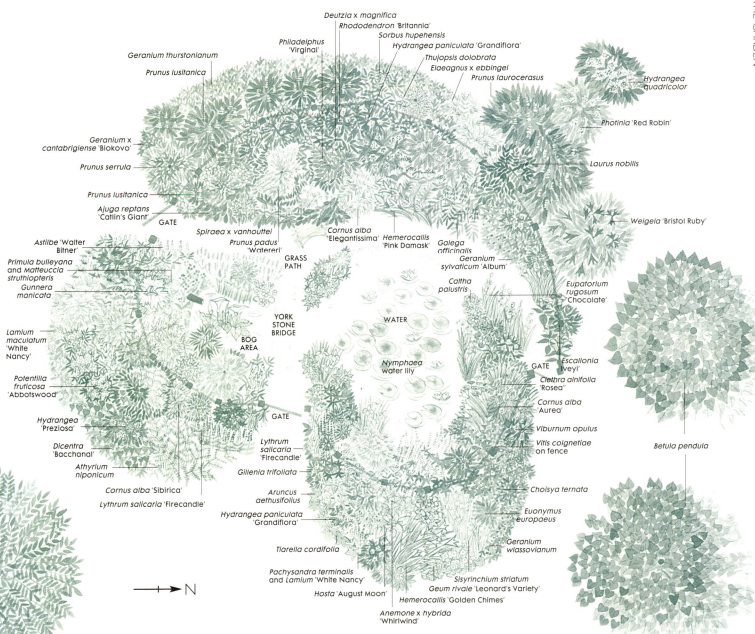

Deutzia x magnifica
Rhododendron 'Britannia'
Sorbus hupehensis
Hydrangea paniculata 'Grandiflora'
Thujopsis dolobrata
Elaeagnus x ebbingei
Prunus laurocerasus
Philadelphus 'Virginal'
Geranium thurstonianum
Prunus lusitanica
Hydrangea quadricolor
Photinia 'Red Robin'
Geranium x cantabrigiense 'Biokovo'
Prunus serrula
Laurus nobilis
Prunus lusitanica
Ajuga reptans 'Catlin's Giant'
GATE
Weigela 'Bristol Ruby'
Spiraea x vanhouttei
Prunus padus 'Watereri'
Cornus alba 'Elegantissima'
Hemerocallis 'Pink Damask'
Galega officinalis
Astilbe 'Walter Bitner'
Geranium sylvaticum 'Album'
GRASS PATH
Primula bulleyana and Matteuccia struthiopteris
Caltha palustris
Gunnera manicata
Eupatorium rugosum 'Chocolate'
Lamium maculatum 'White Nancy'
YORK STONE BRIDGE
BOG AREA
WATER
Potentilla fruticosa 'Abbotswood'
Nymphaea water lily
GATE
Escallonia Iveyi
Clethra alnifolia 'Rosea'
Hydrangea 'Preziosa'
Cornus alba 'Aurea'
GATE
Dicentra 'Bacchanal'
Viburnum opulus
Athyrium niponicum
Lythrum salicaria 'Firecandle'
Vitis coignetiae on fence
Betula pendula
Cornus alba 'Sibirica'
Gillenia trifoliata
Lythrum salicaria 'Firecandle'
Aruncus aethusifolius
Choisya ternata
Hydrangea paniculata 'Grandiflora'
Euonymus europaeus
Tiarella cordifolia
Geranium wlassovianum
Pachysandra terminalis and Lamium 'White Nancy'
Sisyrinchium striatum
Geum rivale 'Leonard's Variety'
Hosta 'August Moon'
Hemerocallis 'Golden Chimes'
Anemone x hybrida 'Whirlwind'

→ N

SPECIAL FEATURES

Perhaps the most difficult task to overcome when erecting fencing around a pond is to create a physical barrier that provides adequate safety while minimizing the visual block that can be created by most forms of fencing.

Traditional post-and-rail was used in this case to blend with the surroundings and the planting. Galvanized chicken wire, which quickly disappears into the background as it oxidizes, provides additional security. It must be remembered that a barrier of this type can only act as a deterrent and is still relatively easy to climb over if someone is determined.

Pathways and gates

The easiest way to fence off a pond would be simply to build a fence all the way round. However, much of the pleasure of a water and bog garden is to get close to it and, without plenty of pathways within the enclosed space, it would only be possible to view the water from over or through the fencing. Therefore, the fence was extended to varying degrees beyond the edges of the water and three gates positioned for access to the pond to minimize the feeling of enclosure.

The gates are linked by a grass path that in places runs right into the water. Not the easiest for maintenance but it gives a very natural effect.

Large dogwoods (*Cornus alba* 'Aurea') are planted either side to reduce the impact of the fence.

A York stone bridge on
steel supports spans the
pond and divides the space
between the deep water
and the planted bog area.

Stone bridge

In order to get even closer to the water, there is a bridge separating the deeper part from
the very shallow area, which creates an environment for marginal and shallow-water plants.
The bridge is constructed of two steel girders and large slabs of reclaimed York stone paving.
The steel supports needed to be set on concrete bases to prevent the bridge from sinking
over time. As reclaimed York stone paving has been used elsewhere in the garden, this
provided some continuity and a span of 3m (10ft) across the water required strong bearers.
Alternatives such as railway sleepers for shorter spans or thick oak timbers could, however,
have been used.

Submersible pump

For a relaxing and gentle sound of running water a submersible pump is installed in the deep
part of the pond, lashed to a pole driven into the bottom of the pond to keep it out of the
mud (remember you cannot do this if you have a liner). The pump is capable of circulating
up to 13,500 litres (3,570 gallons) per hour and is connected to a pipe running along the

bottom of the pond. The water then flows through an old large-diameter cast-iron heating pipe in the shallow water. This keeps the water moving and helps increase the oxygen levels, giving an appearance of natural running water topping up the pond. In this case we fitted a sophisticated solenoid switch and sensor because during the winter months the pond can very quickly flood due to the natural springs nearby. When the level becomes too high, the flow of water is switched to a nearby drainage ditch, keeping the level fairly constant throughout the winter. It is also connected to an underground water supply to keep it topped up in the summer using a similar sensor and solenoid switch.

Seating

This is a secluded area well away from the house and main terrace so it is ideally suited for seating. A good quality oak seat is positioned close to the bridge and the oak will weather to the same colour as the fence and gates surrounding the pond. It is important to ensure the seat is level, both for comfort and appearance, and the bank had to be dug out to facilitate this. The back legs of the bench are in the bed but, as the front sits on the grass, the seat has to be moved for mowing. For level areas it is often more practical to lay paving for the front legs, leaving the back of the bench in the bed on small pads of concrete, brick or paving to stop it from sinking and then to surround it with planting.

The edges of the pond itself slope to varying degrees. Shallow slopes encourage wildlife by enabling them to get in and out, while steeper sides provide a greater depth of water that will not freeze in winter and allows the fish to escape from herons, which need a shallow slope to wade into the water.

Right Planting softens the fencing line on either side. The young birch tree will eventually replace the mature one in the background. In the foreground is *Hydrangea paniculata* 'Grandiflora'.

Below A splash of white is provided by the late-flowering Japanese anemones with tall stems towering above the fence.

PLANTS and PLANTING

To achieve a gentle natural feel with planting, it is essential to create a gradual transition from one area to the next rather than a sharp, sudden contrast. This is particularly important in the situation we have here with barriers of water and fencing. The trick is continuity, and the overall planting theme is to bridge the divide between water, bog and planted beds. So if iris are planted in the shallow water, they should also follow through to the bog area; and where dogwoods are planted on the inside of the fence, they should also be planted on the outside to smooth the transition.

The fence is a relatively heavy structure and structural planting is essential to keep it all in proportion, so the backdrop behind the fence consists of photinia, eleagnus and Portugal laurel, placing the odd one in front of the fence to break the line. Holly has also been used but it must be remembered that most evergreen shrubs will not survive waterlogging. For all-year-round interest in the wet areas a number of dogwoods including *Cornus alba* and *Cornus stolonifera* varieties have been used. These thrive in wet conditions and look superb through the winter with coloured stems of red and yellow. The south-east corner is quite shady until late afternoon due to a large tree, so the planting scheme was contrived to suit partial moist shade as well as sunny, moist conditions.

The lightly variegated leaves of *Cornus alba* 'Elegantissima' contrast with the dark-leafed underplanting of *Ajuga reptans* 'Atropurpurea' and the feathery foliage of the fern *Dryopteris erythrosora*.

Cornus alba **'Elegantissima'** (zones 3–7) has several attributes that provide all-year-round interest. White and green variegated leaves throughout summer are bright and will lighten a dark corner. In autumn they will be tinged with pink before falling and revealing red stems that intensify in colour during winter (see *Cornus alba* 'Sibirica' on page 33 for cultural details). This plant has almost endless possibilities for planting combinations and in the damp areas in which they thrive **Ajuga reptans 'Atropurpurea'** (zones 3–9) is a good underplanting. The rich, dark purple foliage spreads rapidly, hugging the ground, and short spikes of dark blue flowers up to 30cm (12in) appear during early summer and thrive in damp shade.

Astilbe 'Walter Bitner' provides a large clump of late summer colour in a damp corner.

Astilbe **'Walter Bitner'** (zones 3–8) is a recently introduced variety with soft pink plumes of flower and a good compact habit. Astilbe foliage is finely divided, providing an attractive feathery appearance, and varies from light, bright green to bronze in colour depending upon the variety. Astilbes will perform in average light soils but thrive in wet conditions and require a sunny position though will tolerate light shade. The flowers are very showy for a period of 4–6 weeks during mid- to late summer, so it is worth planting earlier flowering perennials such as *Persicaria bistorta* 'Superba' near to the astilbes to ensure a succession of colour.

Clethra alnifolia 'Rosea', with its pale pink, richly scented, bottlebrush-shaped flowers, is a useful late flowering shrub.

The red stems of *Cornus alba* 'Sibirica' provide colour throughout the winter. The underplanting of ferns contrasts well under the leaf canopy during summer.

The white flowers of *Anemone x hybrida* 'Honorine Jobert' held on tall stems continue throughout late summer into autumn.

Clethra alnifolia 'Rosea' (zones 3–9), commonly known as the sweet pepper bush, is a deciduous shrub with an upright habit reaching 2–2.4m (6–8ft) high. The bottlebrush-shaped heads are pale pink and made up of a cluster of small flowers forming a cylindrical shape. These flowers appear during late summer on current season's growth and are very sweetly scented. The foliage turns deep butter yellow in autumn. Soil conditions should be moist yet free draining and this plant is unusual in that it is a late summer flowering shrub that will bloom in shady conditions. It will however perform better in sun or partial shade. The white forms of this plant are more commonly grown than this pink variety.

Cornus alba 'Sibirica' (zones 3–7), also known as *Cornus alba* 'Westonbirt', is the best red-stemmed dogwood and has bright coral bark throughout the winter months. To maintain fresh new growth with good colour, all *Cornus alba* varieties should be pruned to within 5cm (2in) of the previous season's growth every spring. This may seem very drastic but pruning in this way will induce vigour and many shoots will result, forming a multi-stemmed plant. By pruning hard each year the new growth can reach 1.5–2m (5–6ft) in one growing season and the stem colour is more intense. If pruning is neglected, the stem colour fades and the new growth becomes less each year.

Anemone x *hybrida* 'Honorine Jobert' (zones 4–8) is better known as the Japanese anemone. The pure white single flowers with yellow stamens are held on stems 1–1.5m (3–5ft) high, forming a clump up to 1.5m (5ft) wide. The flowers last for up to eight weeks during late summer and early autumn and thrive in full sun or partial shade. The soil conditions should be moist with reasonable drainage as waterlogging in winter could cause rotting of the fibrous roots. There are many other varieties, all either white or pink and varying in height, some with double flowers. They are all capable of naturalizing in ideal conditions.

Butomus umbellatus forms a large, attractive clump in shallow water at the edge of the pond.

The creamy midsummer flowers of *Hydrangea quercifolia* are followed by stunning light and dark red leaves in autumn.

The buttercup-yellow flowers of the marsh marigold, *Caltha palustris*, shine above the dark green leaves.

Butomus umbellatus (zones 3–11) thrives as a marginal plant in full sun and can become quite invasive in the right conditions.
In a small pond it may require reducing every year to prevent it from taking over. However, the multiple flowerheads of soft pink appear over a long period after the narrow, bright green, grassy foliage pierces the water surface, making it a worthwhile plant for most water gardens. It will reach a height of 90–100cm (3ft) above the water surface. The ideal depth of water is 20–30cm (4–5in) and it is easily propagated by division in late spring.

Hydrangea quercifolia (zones 5–9), so called because it has oak tree-like leaves, is a deciduous shrub with large showy heads of white flowers intermittently from early to midsummer. The white flowers slowly change to purplish pink as they mature. It will eventually reach a height of 1.2–1.8m (4–6ft) and spread up to 2.1m (7ft). The large leaves turn vivid reds and oranges in autumn. The branches are quite brittle so it is best grown in a position sheltered from strong winds. Pruning is only necessary to maintain an even shape and should be done after flowering. Grow in full sun or part shade in moist soils.

Caltha palustris (zones 3–7), better known as marsh marigold, thrives in wet soils, typically at the edge of ponds and streams. The rich yellow flowers are dominant in boggy areas during late spring and early summer. This is well before the majority of marginal plants bloom, making it a useful plant to include in the bog garden. It grows to 30–45cm (12–18in) high and wide and prefers full sun for successful flowering, though it is tolerant of light shade. There are also double-flowered and white-flowered varieties worth growing that thrive in the same conditions.

Eupatorium cannabinum 'Flore Pleno' with pale pink fluffy flowers thrives in boggy ground.

Lythrum salicaria 'Firecandle' has tall pink flower spikes. In the background is a dogwood, with some ferns in the lower left corner.

The fluffy white flowers of *Eupatorium rugosum* appear in the background, with *Lysimachia clethroides* in the lower left foreground and *Hosta* 'Royal Standard' in between.

Eupatorium cannabinum **'Flore Pleno'** (zones 4–9) is the double-flowered form of hemp agrimony, which is a weed. However, this form does not self-seed. It simply grows into a larger clump 1.2–1.5m (4–5ft) high with soft rose-coloured fluffy flowers. It grows and associates well close to water and is a very useful late summer flowering bold and lush perennial that requires plenty of space. The flowers attract butterflies and even the dead heads are attractive, remaining well into autumn. It does not normally require staking and is very easy to propagate by division.

Lythrum salicaria **'Firecandle'** (zones 4–9), known as purple loosestrife, thrives in moist boggy areas including the edge of ponds, streams and rivers. This variety is a cultivar of a species naturalized in many areas. The bright pink flowers are on spires that grow up to 1.2m (4ft) high and form a clump 45–60cm (18–24in) wide. It will grow in any moist or very wet soils and will flower best in full sun. The leaves are very similar to the common weed willow herb and can easily be mistaken early in the season. It is therefore advisable to leave a small stump of last year's stems to mark the position over winter rather than cut to the ground at the end of the season.

Lysimachia clethroides (zones 3–8) is a moisture-loving perennial with clusters of starry white flowers in racemes similar to a hebe or veronica but with a curved shape. The flowers appear from late spring through to midsummer above the light green leaves on stems that grow up to 60–90cm (2–3ft). The plant forms a clump that can be quite invasive up to 1.2m (4ft) wide, spreading by underground stems, particularly in fertile, moist soils. The ideal aspect is full sun but it is tolerant of part shade.

SMALL GARDEN
WITH POND

This garden was created to provide a space to relax and dine out of doors surrounded by a wide variety of mass planting. A lawn meanders between the flowerbeds, leading the eye to surrounding countryside with a shelter belt of oak trees in the distance. Closer to the house the planting becomes more intensive and the central feature is a small natural-style pond surrounded by waterside plants, trees and shrubs. The result is a sheltered and secluded haven with expansive views and a garden that blends in with the house and its surroundings.

PLANNING the GARDEN

There were no existing features when this garden was created apart from the single-storey house that stood in open field. A gentle slope towards the house and poor drainage were the obvious features from the outset. A slight frost pocket plus some deer, rabbits and moles only became apparent later!

The three main requirements for this garden were privacy on the road side, maintaining and enhancing views through to the surrounding meadow and allowing for dual-aspect views from the house. There are three main lines of sight: through

a pergola, along the winding lawn with the pond as the focal point in the middle distance and across the pond towards a wildflower meadow. The terrace is regularly used for dining outside throughout the summer months, weather permitting, so the sounds and smells in the garden are an important consideration. As the garden opens to the public for charity twice during the summer, a wide range of plants including some late summer colour is also important.

The pond provides a focal point and the sound of running water is a welcome distraction from traffic noise as well as providing interest and rippling movement on the pond surface. The drystone wall is necessary to retain the bank behind the pond but it also provides a haven for wildlife in the nooks and crannies and also supports growth of mosses and lichens.

The terrace is linked to the pond by a short stretch of lawn, which then meanders around and beyond the borders surrounding the pond, leading the eye towards other areas of the garden. Low maintenance is not a priority though; apart from lawn mowing and edging, the garden can last for long periods with minimum effort. Heavy soils are a problem, however, and attention to ground preparation (see page 132) was, as ever, the most important issue once the layout of the garden had been planned.

When creating an area for privacy there is the danger that you can make the space claustrophobic. This has been avoided by a series of curved beds that creates a vista. At the end of the garden is a small paved area that offers a pleasant view towards the terrace.

Changes in level in this garden are linked by simple brick steps or a sloping lawn and the difference between upper and lower lawn levels is exaggerated by the pond with its drystone wall backdrop. Here and there are 'windows' in the planting, allowing views through to the planting behind the pond and to the meadow beyond. The garden starts off sunny in the morning so, as the day progresses, the pond is gradually shaded by its surrounding planting. It was decided not to plant trees close to the house as in this context they could be oppressive, so shade has to be relied upon from a garden umbrella over the dining area.

Views of the surrounding meadow over perennials and a hedge of *Lonicera nitida*.

SMALL GARDEN
with POND

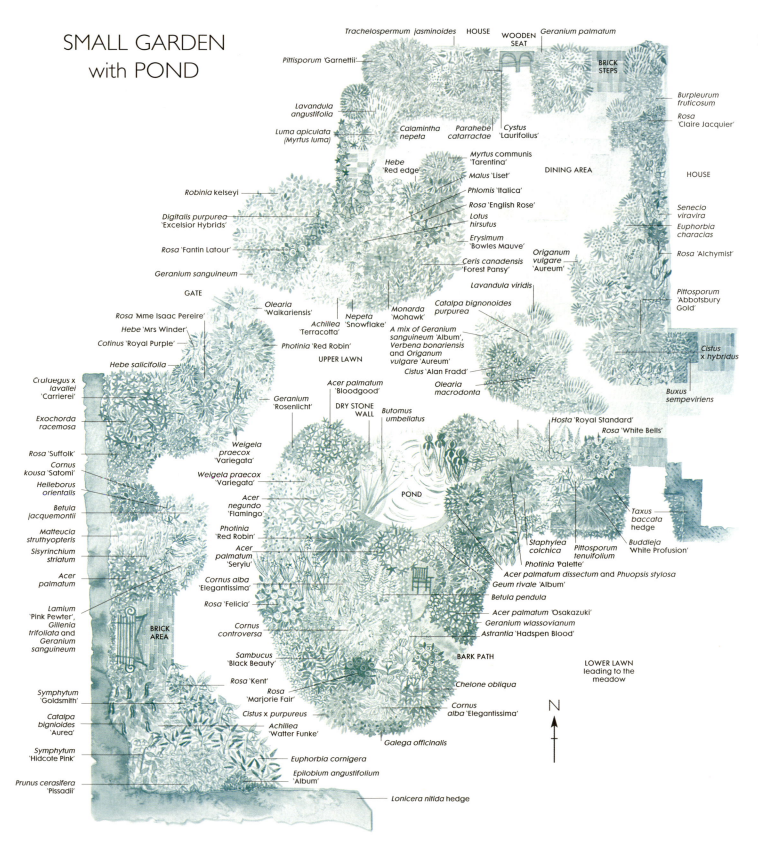

Trachelospermum jasminoides

HOUSE

WOODEN SEAT

Geranium palmatum

Pittisporum 'Garnettii'

BRICK STEPS

Burpleurum fruticosum

Rosa 'Claire Jacquier'

Lavandula angustifolia

Calamintha nepeta

Parahebe catarractae

Cystus 'Laurifolius'

Luma apiculata (Myrtus luma)

Myrtus communis 'Tarentina'

DINING AREA

HOUSE

Hebe 'Red edge'

Malus 'Liset'

Phlomis 'Italica'

Robinia kelseyi

Rosa 'English Rose'

Senecio viravira

Digitalis purpurea 'Excelsior Hybrids'

Lotus hirsutus

Euphorbia characias

Erysimum 'Bowles Mauve'

Rosa 'Alchymist'

Rosa 'Fantin Latour'

Ceris canadensis 'Forest Pansy'

Origanum vulgare 'Aureum'

Geranium sanguineum

Lavandula viridis

Pittosporum 'Abbotsbury Gold'

GATE

Olearia 'Waikariensis'

Nepeta 'Snowflake'

Monarda 'Mohawk'

Catalpa bignonoides purpurea

Rosa 'Mme Isaac Pereire'

Achillea 'Terracotta'

Cistus x hybridus

Hebe 'Mrs Winder'

A mix of Geranium sanguineum 'Album', Verbena bonariensis and Origanum vulgare 'Aureum'

Cotinus 'Royal Purple'

Photinia 'Red Robin'

UPPER LAWN

Hebe salicifolia

Buxus sempeviriens

Cistus 'Alan Fradd'

Crataegus x lavallei 'Carrierei'

Acer palmatum 'Bloodgood'

Olearia macrodonta

Geranium 'Rosenlicht'

DRY STONE WALL

Butomus umbellatus

Hosta 'Royal Standard'

Exochorda racemosa

Rosa 'White Bells'

Rosa 'Suffolk'

Weigela praecox 'Variegata'

Cornus kousa 'Satomi'

Weigela praecox 'Variegata'

POND

Helleborus orientalis

Acer negundo 'Flamingo'

Taxus baccata hedge

Betula jacquemontii

Photinia 'Red Robin'

Staphylea colchica

Matteucia struthyopteris

Pittosporum tenuifolium

Buddleja 'White Profusion'

Sisyrinchium striatum

Acer palmatum 'Seryiu'

Photinia 'Palette'

Acer palmatum

Cornus alba 'Elegantissima'

Acer palmatum dissectum and Phuopsis stylosa

Rosa 'Felicia'

Geum rivale 'Album'

Lamium 'Pink Pewter', Gillenia trifoliata and Geranium sanguineum

Betula pendula

Cornus controversa

Acer palmatum 'Osakazuki'

Geranium wlassovianum

BRICK AREA

Astrantia 'Hadspen Blood'

Sambucus 'Black Beauty'

BARK PATH

Symphytum 'Goldsmith'

Rosa 'Kent'

Chelone obliqua

LOWER LAWN leading to the meadow

Catalpa bignioides 'Aurea'

Rosa 'Marjorie Fair'

Cistus x purpureus

Cornus alba 'Elegantissima'

Symphytum 'Hidcote Pink'

Achillea 'Watter Funke'

N

Galega officinalis

Prunus cerasifera 'Pissadii'

Euphorbia cornigera

Epilobium angustifolium 'Album'

Lonicera nitida hedge

SPECIAL FEATURES

It is good to have a pond that wildlife can easily crawl in and out of instead of jumping off a precipice and struggling to climb steep walls to avoid drowning. With this small natural style of pond the lawn drifts gently into the water. On this small scale it can be difficult to achieve water deep enough to sustain pond life through cold periods and maintain a body of water large enough to remain viable throughout hot periods.

In order to achieve both requirements the pond is dug into a gentle slope and a drystone wall rises straight up from the water at the back, creating two level areas where once there was a gentle fall. Effectively this is terracing but in a more subtle way and has provided more interest to the garden as well as the additional feature of a body of water in which to grow aquatics and marginals.

It is rare to dig a small pond and find that it retains water without the use of a liner. In this case a butyl liner was laid over a layer of protective matting in a hole gradually sloping from natural ground level at the front to approximately 1m (3½ft) deep at the back.

Taking care not to puncture the liner, a drystone wall was then constructed on top of the liner to retain the bank. (It is best to place some matting on top of the liner on which to build the wall.) In this case sandstone was used as it is the local stone and associates well with local brick and tiling materials. It is always better to use a local material if possible; the chances are it will be more sympathetic with the surroundings, including houses and outbuildings. The sandstone in this case readily supports mosses and lichens, which enhance the appearance over a short period of time.

When the stonework was completed, more matting was laid on top of the liner, then a layer of clay-based soil was put in the bottom of the pond that hide the liner and provide a support system for plants and wildlife. The soil ideally should be sterilized and low in organic matter. If the soil contains compost it will decompose and the water will become very unpleasant. It should also be free of stones. (Useful tip: ram some hoggin, type 1, or similar material under the pond liner where the lawn is to meet the water to prevent the edge from collapsing if walked upon. The grass should still survive as it will draw moisture from the pond. Ensure the liner is protected from this hard material by some thick matting.) The grass close to the water's edge may always have to be hand clipped using shears, or strimmed. It will not be safe to mow close to the water,

Above Th lawn runs right up to the water's edge.

Left *Geranium* 'Rosenlicht' flows either side of the meandering lawn. A silver birch tree frames the view to *Catalpa bignonioides* 'Aurea' in the distance.

Right Planting behind the pond is illuminated at night with carefully positioned garden lighting.

especially if your lawnmower is electric. The result here was a pond approximately 3.5x4m (11½x13ft) with varying depth from just a few centimetres to 80cm (2½ft).

Water pump

For the sound of running water and to assist oxygenation, a submersible pump circulates water from a position on a stone slab in the deepest part of the pond through a pipe fed between the liner and stone wall. The pump has an output of about 300 litres (66 gallons) per hour and is sufficient to send the water gently cascading over a piece of sandstone that protrudes from the side wall. Using a 'dirty water pump' means it will not have a filter that needs cleaning. In addition to the sound it also creates a nice rippling effect across the water. It must be remembered that natural ponds are seldom clear, though this one did clear eventually after about a year until fish were introduced and it has remained muddy ever since.

Atmospheric lighting

This is an ideal setting for garden lighting as the garden is always on view from everywhere inside the house. The lighting was carefully positioned to catch the gentle running water

and rippling pond surface. Further uplighting within the surrounding planting gives a tremendous impression of depth and creates a sense of atmosphere at night that is particularly pleasing when viewed from inside the house or when sitting outside on the terrace on a warm summer evening.

Paving

The paving was laid using new York stone with a brick edge. Natural stone will weather whereas concrete can remain the same colour as the day it was laid. Even so, good quality concrete paving could have been used here and would have been equally appropriate with this modern house. As the paved areas are relatively small, a brick edge gives definition and ties in the paving with the house walls and brick steps.

An important construction detail is the lawn level, which is just above the paving level for ease of mowing. The shape of the terrace allows for easy planting in the flowerbeds next to the house with ample room for table and chairs. It is important to bear in mind that, if the furniture is to be removed for storage during winter, a vast expanse of paving might not be very attractive to look out on for six months of the year. A few carefully positioned pots alleviate the stark appearance and these can be positioned in the corners produced by the stepped shape of the terrace. The stepped shaped edges also create an interesting space for planting and provide a flowing pathway. Cutting angular paving into a curve does not give a good appearance. It is far better to step the path and let the planting provide the flowing curves.

Above The edge of the York stone paved terrace is defined by a brick edge with the lawn flush or just above the paving for easy mowing.

Left An ancient oak bench smothered by grapevine *Vitis* 'Brant' and *Geranium palmatum*.

Furniture is chosen for comfort and to link the modern style of house with traditional garden surroundings, hence a wooden table and chairs with timber treatment, sympathetic with the timber cladding of the house. A seating area has been created in front of the main windows and an ancient oak bench positioned under the eaves in the hope that it will last another century or two, protected from the weather. It is important to remember in any type of garden that the structural features are there to support a wide range of planting and should therefore be subtle and not too dominant.

A summer's day on the terrace surrounded by planting and with a view of the birch trees beyond at the end of the meandering lawn.

PLANTS and PLANTING

There were no established plants in this garden which was previously field. The soil is heavy clay with good clay loam above and poor winter drainage due to surface compaction and a plough pan (see page 132). The soil improvement carried out was mainly decompaction and the incorporation of plenty of mushroom compost and sharp sand. In winter, surface water is slow to dissipate and in summer, cracks open up that are large enough to lose your trowel. On heavy clay soils in summer when cracks appear, rake as much sharp washed sand as possible into the cracks. This will improve winter drainage.

The planting was designed to create a sense of seclusion with impact during summer and early autumn. I wanted to include a wide range of plants while maintaining continuity and unity despite the varied growing conditions of sun and shade, dry and boggy.

Instant summer screening was achieved with silver birch, *Betula utilis jacquemontii*, which also provides a light canopy for the shade-loving groundcover of *Symphytum ibericum*, *Geranium macrorrhizum* and *Lamium* 'Pink Pewter'. These associate well with the bog and marginal plants that flow gently down towards the pond. *Cornus alba* 'Elegantissima' and *Hosta* 'Royal Standard' thrive in the damp areas and hardy geraniums soften the transition from damp shade to dry sunloving plants closer to the house. A further sense of seclusion is provided by surrounding the terrace with planting, engulfing the paved corners and cladding the walls with climbers.

The silver variegation of *Cornus alternifolia* 'Argentea' stands out above an underplanting of *Hosta* 'Royal Standard' at the edge of the pond.

Euphorbia cornigera in the foreground with a background of spiky white *Epilobium angustifolium* 'Album'. Beyond is a hay meadow full of ox-eyed daisies.

Cornus alternifolia **'Argentea'** (zones 3–7), although planted near the pond in this situation, requires well-drained yet moisture-retentive soil. This large shrub will eventually reach a height of 3m (10ft) and produces small creamy white flowers in flat heads held above the layered stems during early summer. The silvery white variegated-leafed branches spread in elegant tiers that act as supports for tall thin-stemmed perennials, such as *Eupatorium aromaticum* and the flowers of *Hosta* 'Royal Standard'. The white variegated leaves contrast with surrounding dark green planting and perennial underplanting of *Cornus canadensis*, *Lysimachia clethroides* and *Geranium wlassovianum*.

Euphorbia cornigera (zones 7–9) has bright green foliage with distinctive veining and limegreen, brightening to golden yellow, flowers in early summer. It must have full sun and will grow to 3ft (90cm) high. As with all euphorbias, the sap is toxic and can cause a rash and severe eye irritation so wear long sleeves and gloves when working with or close to this plant. *Epilobium angustifolium* **'Album'** (zones 7–8) is a white form of the invasive willowherb also know as fireweed. Slightly less invasive than the common pink-flowered variety, it will nevertheless reach a height of 1.2m (4ft) and spread by underground stems, so give it plenty of room.

A foreground of *Weigela praecox* 'Variegata' contrasts with the dark leaves of *Hebe salicifolia* behind and the *Continus coggygria* 'Royal Purple' and rambling rose 'Leontine Gervais' in the background.

Catalpa bignonoides 'Aurea' forms a spreading canopy over groundcover *Rosa* 'Kent'.

Achillea 'Walter Funke' prolongs the season of colour associated with the golden catalpa during late summer.

Weigela praecox 'Variegata' (zones 4–8), once established, forms an attractive mound of variegated foliage. Initially the variegation is yellowish before becoming white. For best results, last year's stems should be removed as soon as the pale pink flowers are finished in early summer to encourage new growth from the base of the plant. This will maintain a bush of up to 1.5m (5ft) with a framework of young branches. It is of weaker constitution than the more widely grown *Weigela florida* 'Variegata' but is of softer, more subtle habit, texture and colour. *Geranium* 'Rosenlicht' and *Dicentra* 'Bountiful' are good for underplanting this weigela and the dark green and red leaves of *Photinia* 'Red Robin' are a good contrast.

Catalpa bignonoides 'Aurea' (zones 4–8), the golden-leafed Indian bean tree, forms a large canopy of heart-shaped leaves that are lime green in early summer, becoming increasingly yellow. Catalpa is one of the last trees to burst into leaf, often as late as early summer. This is followed by the snapdragon-like white-speckled pink flowers later on. It is a tree that can easily be contained in size by pruning hard, though if pruned it will put on very vigorous, lush and colourful growth and perhaps less flower. It is planted in this garden to form an umbrella over the seating area. Avoid windy situations as the leaves are very large and easily damaged. Underplanting the catalpa and blending subtly with the lime-green leaves above are *Symphytum* 'Goldsmith' with soft green and yellow leaves.

Achillea 'Walter Funke' (zones 3–8) provides a useful splash of colour during mid- to late summer. There have been many new introductions of achillea, a form of yarrow, in recent years and the range includes soft reds, mauves and buffs as well as the old favourites in bright yellow. Achilleas normally need some staking but can be grown close to the base of a branching shrub to provide support. They require well-drained soil otherwise they are prone to root death in winter, but keep well watered during summer to avoid mildew attack. When achilleas have finished flowering, cut down the stems close to ground level, allowing the rosette of new leaves to develop and sometimes they will produce another crop of short flowering stems later in the season.

Betula utilis var. *jacquemontii* provides shade for ferns planted underneath. Lower branches can be removed as the tree develops to reveal more of the stunning white trunk.

The shuttlecock fern *Matteucia struthiopteris,* with its light green foliage, surrounded by *Geranium macrorrhizum* 'Bevans Variety'.

The dark red clusters of *Rosa* 'Marjorie Fair' emerge through the silvery variegated leaves of *Cornus alba* 'Elegantissima', while the purple leaves of *Sambucus* 'Black Beauty' contrast with surrounding foliage.

Betula utilis var. *jacquemontii* (zones 2–6) is one of the most popular of the white-stemmed birches with a more rigid habit than the common silver birch. They provide a light canopy allowing plenty of underplanting, have attractive silver, white, pink or black peeling trunks for year-round colour and are quick growing yet do not reach enormous proportions. Because of the availability in large sizes, I planted a group to form a quick screen. The ground here is wet during winter and birch thrive in moist soils. Birch trees over 1.5m (5ft) tall do not transplant easily, so avoid bare-rooted trees. Rootballed trees are normally successful but container-grown specimens are a safer choice.

Matteucia struthiopteris (zones 3–7) is the shuttlecock fern, so called because of its shape in early spring when the fronds are vertical and knitted lightly at the top. At this stage they are at their most attractive. Matteucia requires shade and very moist soil, thriving in boggy conditions. By midsummer the leaves are rather flattened and less attractive, but they turn a golden yellow colour in autumn. In front of the ferns is *Geranium macrorrhizum* 'Bevans Variety' (zones 3–7), an evergreen groundcover geranium with scented leaves and rich pink flowers in late spring and early summer that thrives in shady conditions. Most geraniums are easily propagated by division but the macrorrhizum varieties have creeping stems rather than being clump forming and are less easy to divide.

Rosa 'Marjorie Fair' (zones 5–9) is an easy variety of shrub rose to grow and is free flowering with a continuation of raspberry-coloured flowers throughout the summer. It has an eventual height and spread of 1.5m (5ft) and is disease resistant. As with all roses, the roots are kept moist. The flower colour associates well with the dark foliage of *Sambucus* 'Black Beauty', a form of elder, which should be pruned hard each winter to within a few centimetres of the previous year's growth to maintain the intense leaf colour and contrast with the light variegated leaves of the neighbouring *Cornus alba* 'Elegantissima' (see page 32).

Cercis 'Forest Pansy' provides a dark contrast to the purplish fluffy flowers of Monarda 'Mohawk'.

The green lavender Lavandula viridis creates a lovely lime-green contrast for use with a variety of other darker-leaved plants.

The flat flowerheads of Achillea 'Terracotta', fading to pale yellow, are emphasized by spiky, glaucous blue grass Koeleria glauca.

Cercis 'Forest Pansy' (zones 5–9) is the purple form of Judas tree that has very striking ruby red, heart-shaped leaves following pale pink flowers on bare stems in early summer. It can grow slowly to 8m (25ft) high and although very hardy is rather prone to damage by late frosts, killing the new shoots and causing dieback that must be pruned out immediately. Plant in an open, sunny position with shelter from strong winds for good results. The soft purplish flowers of Monarda 'Mohawk' (zones 4–8) associate well with the cercis and provide some late summer colour. Monarda requires moist soil to thrive and is rather prone to mildew, though this variety is supposed to be mildew resistant.

Lavandula viridis (zone 8), the green French lavender, is a highly scented variety with light green leaves and large heads of green and white flowers. This versatile colouring allows it to be used in many combinations. Although rather tender it has survived for several seasons in this garden, which is surprising as the heavy soil is not ideal for this rather delicate lavender. In this situation I have used it to mark the corners of the paving. This lavender combines well with Origanum 'Aureum' and Crocosmia 'Solfaterre'.

Achillea 'Terracotta' (zones 3–8) is a recent introduction, providing midsummer colour that lends itself to a range of combinations. Here, the colour has faded and, more by accident rather than design, it provides an interesting combination with the blue grass Koeleria glauca – a good example to illustrate that the variations and combinations are endless and often provide nice surprises. Koeleria glauca (zones 5–9) is a perennial grass with short grey leaves reaching 30–40cm (12–15in) high. It requires a warm sheltered position and good drainage.

COURTYARD AND FORMAL GARDEN

This garden in a glorious country setting has a combination of wide open spaces with far-reaching views and cosy, sheltered corners. The property and surroundings are traditional in style and have a strong historical atmosphere. Good quality, natural materials and strong structural planting are essential to reflect the powerful structure of the house. The house has an air of permanence and the garden should reflect this sense of longevity, even though much of the planting is still only five or six years old. The evergreen structure means that the predominant colour is green throughout the year and any colourful planting is contained within the green framework of foliage.

PLANNING the GARDEN

The three main elements to this garden are a large terrace, a formal walk down to an ancient moat and, around the corner, a small shady courtyard. At the planning stage the terrace was a tarmac drive sweeping around the house, allowing vehicles to come right up to the back door. There was a retaining wall forming a raised bed at the corner of the house that served no real purpose and access to the moat was across an undulating lawn.

With views from the house across this area to the moat and to the parkland beyond, it was important to maintain open space. However, it was also necessary to create a strong shape and structure to the garden so that it remains in balance with the large, timbered house. The house has an atmosphere of history and tranquillity, combined with the wonderful quality of materials and craftsmanship from long ago, and it proved challenging to make radical changes to the garden that would be in keeping with the property.

Removing the drive was an easy decision and therefore the first place to start the layout plan. Next, it was necessary to plot the pathways and establish the key areas for planting. The natural routes for paths were easy to see and places for tall plants dictated by the important views from the house. An old privy building in a dilapidated state lay in one corner and this had to be incorporated into the new layout or removed. As part of the history of the property and because it was constructed of attractive old bricks, it was an easy decision to retain it but not for its original purpose.

Planting has to be bold with a property of this scale. The *Wisteria sinensis* clambering up the chimneys helps unify the house and garden. The box and the choisyia are strong forms consistent with the strong lines of the building.

The soil in this garden is a sandy loam over a soft sandstone and is a dark reddish brown in colour. It is very free draining and yet soaks up water quickly, becoming very sticky during wet periods, when it should not be walked upon. Regular mulching with leaf mould or some well-rotted manure is required to retain moisture during summer and top up the nutrient levels.

The aspect is open and sunny in the terrace and moat area with the small courtyard in total shade for most of the day. Summers can be very hot and winter temperatures can fall to below −10°C (50°F), sometimes for over a week, with strong winds cutting across the surrounding open countryside.

The planting scheme aims to be bold, unfussy, with strong structure and requiring minimal maintenance. It is essential to have bold planting in association with a house such as this. However, in addition the owners wanted plenty of interest all year round. The architectural structure of the garden was given shape with a large proportion of evergreens in groups that provide a strong backbone to the garden in winter and create a contrasting backdrop to flowers during spring and summer.

The existing planting was mainly structural with a large yew hedge to the east and a shelter belt of laurel and sycamore to the west. A large wisteria clothed the brick chimney breast and a pyracantha covered a large part of the house wall. Two large conifers and a group of *Viburnum mariesii* were the only existing planting between the house and the section of moat.

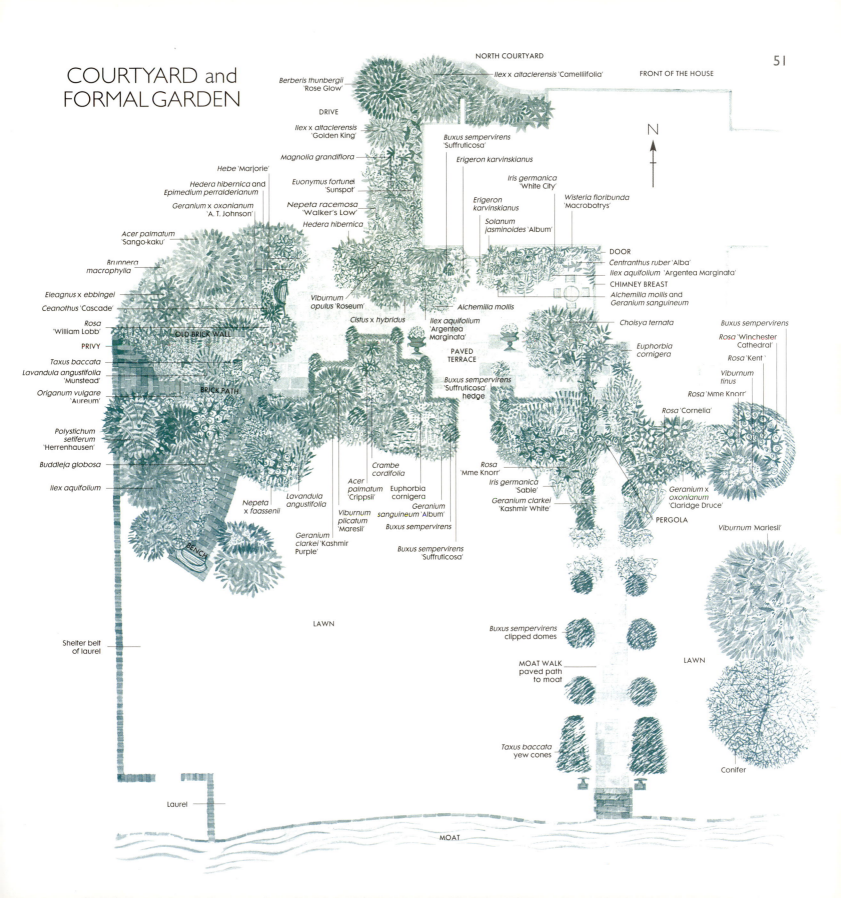

COURTYARD and
FORMAL GARDEN

NORTH COURTYARD

FRONT OF THE HOUSE

Ilex x *altaclerensis* 'Camelliifolia'

Berberis thunbergii 'Rose Glow'

N

DRIVE

Buxus sempervirens 'Suffruticosa'

Ilex x *altaclerensis* 'Golden King'

Erigeron karvinskianus

Magnolia grandiflora

Iris germanica 'White City'

Hebe 'Marjorie'

Euonymus fortunei 'Sunspot'

Erigeron karvinskianus

Wisteria floribunda 'Macrobotrys'

Hedera hibernica and *Epimedium perralderianum*

Nepeta racemosa 'Walker's Low'

Solanum jasminoides 'Album'

Geranium x *oxonianum* 'A. T. Johnson'

Hedera hibernica

DOOR

Centranthus ruber 'Alba'

Acer palmatum 'Sango-kaku'

Ilex aquifolium 'Argentea Marginata'

Brunnera macrophylla

CHIMNEY BREAST

Viburnum opulus 'Roseum'

Alchemilla mollis

Alchemilla mollis and *Geranium sanguineum*

Eleagnus x *ebbingei*

Cistus x *hybridus*

Ilex aquifolium 'Argentea Marginata'

Choisya ternata

Buxus sempervirens

Ceanothus 'Cascade'

Rosa 'Winchester Cathedral'

Rosa 'William Lobb'

OLD BRICK WALL

PAVED TERRACE

Euphorbia cornigera

Rosa 'Kent'

PRIVY

Taxus baccata

Viburnum tinus

Lavandula angustifolia 'Munstead'

BRICK PATH

Buxus sempervirens 'Suffruticosa' hedge

Rosa 'Mme Knorr'

Origanum vulgare 'Aureum'

Rosa 'Cornelia'

Polystichum setiferum 'Herrenhausen'

Crambe cordifolia

Rosa 'Mme Knorr'

Buddleja globosa

Acer palmatum 'Crippsii'

Euphorbia cornigera

Iris germanica 'Sable'

Geranium x *oxonianum* 'Claridge Druce'

Ilex aquifolium

Geranium sanguineum 'Album'

Geranium clarkei 'Kashmir White'

Nepeta x *faassenii*

Lavandula angustifolia

Buxus sempervirens

PERGOLA

Viburnum 'Mariesii'

Viburnum plicatum 'Maresii'

Geranium clarkei 'Kashmir Purple'

Buxus sempervirens 'Suffruticosa'

BENCH

LAWN

Buxus sempervirens clipped domes

LAWN

Shelter belt of laurel

MOAT WALK paved path to moat

Taxus baccata yew cones

Conifer

Laurel

MOAT

SPECIAL FEATURES

Right An oak pergola links the moat walk with the main terrace and graduates the height from house to garden. It also provides a shady area to sit on a hot summer's day.

Below This sheltered corner is dominated by wisteria on the chimney breast. To the left is a cone-shaped variegated holly underplanted with *Stachys lanata* to soften the edge of the paving.

All the features in this garden had to be related to the house, which naturally dominates. It is a half-timbered manor house with dramatic ancient chimneys towering above the rooftop. The garden terrace built in slabs of high-quality reclaimed York stone replaces an earlier tarmac drive and narrows down to the side of the property with planting on either side to provide some privacy from the remaining drive and parking area.

Paving and planting

To soften the edges of the paving, generous planting areas are maintained close to the house, allowing for planting to flow over the edges and to clothe the walls. The paving runs up to the base of the huge chimney breast, leaving the weathered stone clearly visible and providing sheltered space for a table and chairs just outside the door. At one side of the chimney breast is an established specimen of *Choisya ternata*, providing a good evergreen background and scented flowers. All corners of the terrace have pockets for planting thyme, alchemilla, santolina and other spreading plants, which allows the terrace, although a large area, to retain a sense of proportion within the setting without appearing to be a vast expanse of stone. The joints have dry, coarse mortar brushed in to hold the slabs firm and yet allow plants to self-seed in them.

Oak pergola

Leading around the chimney breast to the moat walk, the path is covered by an oak pergola that helps to unify the garden with the timbered part of the house as well as provide a structure for climbing and rambling roses. This softens the corner of the house wall and creates a cosy space to sit in this transitional area. It also provides a focal point from the other side of the terrace and when looking back from the moat. Here the timbers are 15cm (5in) square section and the structure extends beyond the end of the house.

Pathways

The paving continues as a path leading to the moat with clipped box domes on either side. The edges of the path are indented to allow space for these domes and links both parts of the garden either side as well as in the direction the path leads. All too often a path slices up space in a garden and spoils the flow of the lawn. With the layout here, the lawn runs between the box domes up to the path, making it possible to step off on to the lawn at any stage yet still leading in one direction. The series of box domes is repeated right down to the end of the

The path along the
moat walk links many
of the focal points
of the garden and
allows access from all
directions. The position
of the box domes
either side of the
path generates views
from every angle.

path, which is punctuated at the end with a large yew cone on each side. The box domes are echoed in other parts of the garden with box cones (*Buxus sempervirens*) either side of the steps opposite the main doors and low box hedges (*Buxus suffruticosa*) around the main beds. These are clipped once or twice a year in early summer and sometimes at the end of the summer too. At strategic points, cones of holly are positioned to continue this topiary theme. Variegated holly cones are planted in the beds close to the house to echo the white walls of the house. The box and holly ensure a good strong framework is present throughout the year and is especially prominent during the winter months, acting in a supporting role for the summer colour.

Simple steps in the local sandstone lead down to the moat and strategically placed staddle stones mark the end of the path. These mushroom-shaped staddle stones were originally intended to support a granary building, carrying it off the ground to ensure the grain was kept dry. The wide, overhanging tops prevented mice and rats from running up the walls and getting into the granary. Today they make good garden features if positioned carefully.

Restored original features

On the other side of the terrace a wall was built approximately 1.5m (5ft) high to provide extra shelter and privacy. This linked to an existing wall, bringing it closer to the house. Old bricks were used and the top capped with reclaimed, local round-topped coping stones; a lime mortar was used to maintain the rustic appearance of all the walls on the property. At the far end of this wall, at the end of the path, is the old privy that was restored to become an attractive brick feature with a clay tile roof on which to grow rambling roses and climbers such as trachelospermum and clematis.

The path leading to the privy is in old brick and incorporates a step. Level changes are often difficult to deal with but, by keeping the main terrace all on one level, it was necessary only to have a few shallow steps at the points where one area leads to the next. Using bricks allowed for gentle curves where rectangular slabs would need to have been laid in stepped fashion and cut square slabs rarely look right. Low drystone walls using the local sandstone were constructed only where necessary to allow for level changes and these never exceed 30cm (12in) high and are softened with planting.

Driveway

A section of decorative wrought-iron park railing engulfed by *Viburnum opulus* 'Roseum' in the background with evergreen *Euonymus* 'Goldspot', groundcover ivy and *Alchemilla mollis* in front.

Leading round the house on the west side several attractive decorative wrought-iron park railing sections provide a subtle boundary to the main terrace, giving way to the tarmac drive before leading to the north courtyard on a dark blue/black engineering brick path. A very attractive open oak porch is the main feature here and the layout and planting is kept very simple for low maintenance with a solid and bold planting scheme. The best way to plant against such strong and dominant features, which here also included a thick 1.8m (6ft) high stone wall, is to use a few varieties of strong and dominant plants. Variegated or feathery leaves are too fussy so dark green is best and, in this shady position, a yew hedge was ideal. Planted along the base of the wall in a very narrow bed, it will be kept to only about 1m (3ft) tall. For continuity it also leads up the steps on either side to be clipped in a low banister shape, reducing the impact of the steps in a very simple yet effective manner. York stone slabs were the main hard surface with a path leading through in the dark blue/black engineering bricks. Normally I would allow the path to form the edge of the beds but, in this case, small local sandstone blocks were ideal as they are nicely weathered and echo the stone wall on the other side. This whole area is very low maintenance and carefully designed to look good all year round.

A range of clipped yew and box creates varied form and texture in this narrow bed at the base of the porch. *Pachysandra terminalis* and *Euonymus* 'Emerald Gaiety' spill over on to the path.

PLANTS and PLANTING

There were few existing plants to incorporate into this planting scheme, save for a pyracantha on the house wall with a well-established wisteria on the chimney breast and *Choisya ternata* at the base of the chimney. The brief was to provide a low-maintenance structured planting with a traditional appearance using predominantly blue and white flowers in the area close to the terrace. Box edging, *Buxus suffruticosa,* was used to enclose the beds by the terrace and plenty of topiary box punctuates the junction of paths, steps and lawn. In beds surrounding the house, a planting of alchemilla and geraniums that has been allowed to spread over the paving and the terrace is further softened by alchemilla and erigeron self-seeded in between the slabs. Box topiary unifies the whole planting scheme, enhanced by the formal structure of cones of variegated holly, *Ilex argentea* 'Marginata', to provide year-round form and colour.

The overall effect is a strong evergreen structure within which softer planting flows, providing colour that is ever changing with the seasons. During winter there are many shades of green, provided mainly by the box and yew. For the summer, some pinks and purples have crept into the blue-and-white planting in the form of roses on and around the pergola.

The lime-green leaves of *Origanum vulgare* 'Aureum' light up the planting at the base of the old privy against a background of *Euphorbia wulfenii* and *Artemisia abrotanum.*

Origanum vulgare 'Aureum' (zones 4–8) is a golden form of the herb oregano or marjoram. It has a low spreading habit 20–30cm (6–12in) high by 45–60cm (18–24in) wide, forming a dense mat of roots and shoots. The aromatic leaves start off lime green in colour and become bright yellow if in full sun. Purplish pink flowers appear above the foliage during late summer. Good drainage is essential for this plant to overwinter successfully and it will withstand drought conditions. It is useful for edges of borders if planted in small drifts and associates well with glaucous and lime-green plants such as *Euphorbia wulfenii, Ballota* 'Allhallows Green' and *Lavandula viridis.* The golden leaves also look good with the white flowers and greyish foliage of *Nepeta* 'Snowflake' or contrasting with the blue catmint, *Nepeta mussinii.* It is a versatile little plant, useful in many combinations.

Buxus domes on the moat walk are echoed around the garden and mark the position of pathways, steps and individual areas.

Buxus sempervirens (zones 5–6) is the most common box to be grown for hedging and topiary. If left to grow full size it can slowly reach 6m (20ft) high, though is rarely seen above 2.5m (8ft) high. There are many forms: dome shape, upright, dwarf, even weeping. The species and its forms are adaptable to most well-drained soils and do best in a rich, fertile ground. They are very shallow rooting, which can be useful where soil depth is limited, and they will benefit from a regular light mulch of compost. The growth is naturally bushy but regular clipping to form the required shape maintains compact growth and should be carried out during summer. Trim after the danger of frost has passed – early summer in most areas – as it will remove any frosted tips and encourage a bushy habit. Hard pruning encourages strong growth.

The white flowers on dark green foliage of *Rosa* 'Kent' mixed with *Geranium sanguineum* 'Album' provide delicate white edging to the lawn in the terrace beds.

The terrace has plants growing here and there within the paving away from the heavily trodden areas. *Parahebe catarractae* (centre) forms a small dome shape covered with pale blue flowers.

The white flowers of *Malus* 'Dartmouth' dominate this scene in late spring. To the left are creamy white layered branches of *Vibernum* 'Mariesii'.

Rosa 'Kent' (zones 5–9) is a low-growing shrub rose, one of the 'county series', and grows to 45cm (18in) high and 1m (3ft) wide. The white, semi-double flowers appear continually from spring into autumn above dark green leaves. Although it can get black spot it is one of the more disease-resistant hybrids I have grown. *Geranium sanguineum* 'Album' (zones 4–8) is a versatile plant for a whole range of combinations due to the plain dark green leaves and clear white flowers. It should be used in drifts, particularly at the edge of beds, and will serve either to tone down fussy white variegated plants and strong colours or lighten dull areas. Best in full sun and fertile well-drained soil, it grows to 30x45cm (12x18in) and can be cut back after the first main flowering to encourage a fresh flush of growth and flower.

Parahebe catarractae (zones 8–10) is a slightly tender evergreen shrub that forms a low, dense mound 30x60cm (1x2ft). The flowers are small, blue (there is also a white form) and saucer shaped, appearing all summer. It is a useful plant for the edge of borders, particularly in corners of paved areas where it will spread and soften the edge of paving. It is also good for containers, acting as the anchor plant around which seasonal planting of either bulbs, black violas or, for winter colour, small variegated ivy may be planted.

Malus 'Dartmouth' (zones 4–8) is a cultivar of the crab apple tree that is ideal for small gardens as well as larger ones, growing to a maximum of 4m (12ft). During late spring and early summer the tree is a cloud of white flowers before the leaves appear. For the summer months it looks much like any other small apple tree and by autumn small, glowing bright red apples appear that remain on the tree often after the leaves have fallen. It has a light canopy and rounded head that can easily be pruned to shape if necessary during the winter months. All malus prefer a heavy soil with an open aspect. This variety is fairly disease resistant but should be kept watered during periods of drought otherwise mildew and apple scab can be a problem.

A tapestry of plants on the edge of the terrace includes a pleasing combination of the pink flowers of *Geranium sanguineum* with the lime-green blooms of *Alchemilla mollis*.

All along the path *Alchemilla mollis* blurs the join between path and bed and is busily seeding itself in the cracks.

Clipped domes and cones of box (*Buxus*) dominate the beds surrounding the terrace and are linked by the continuous edge of *Buxus suffruticosa*, which will provide constant interest and structure all year.

Geranium sanguineum (zones 4–8), known as the bloody cranesbill, is an easily grown hardy geranium forming a mound 30–45cm (12–18in) high with similar spread. It has dark green leaves and magenta pink flowers that continue all summer. If the plant becomes straggly partway through the season, cut back hard and it will regrow and flower until autumn. Best grown in full sun, it thrives in well-drained fertile ground and will tolerate poor soils. It is a useful plant for edges of borders and will combine with many varied planting schemes. The dark leaves and purplish tinge to the flowers lend themselves to a whole range of planting partners such as *Cistus* x *purpureus*, *Weigela praecox* 'Variegata' or floribunda *Rosa* 'English Miss', or with the earlier flowering *Dicentra* 'Luxuriant', *Alchemilla mollis* or *Nepeta mussinii*.

Alchemilla mollis (zones 3–8), also known as lady's mantle, is sometimes considered a weed. However, with attractive lime-green flowers and pretty, rounded, grey-green wavy leaves it is a very underrated garden plant. It will thrive in almost any conditions except boggy areas and associates easily with a whole range of colours: blue, white, silver, yellow. Plant in drifts on the edge of paths or in repetitive clumps. *Alchemilla* readily self-seeds and looks good when it has scattered itself in beds, gravel paths and cracks in paving. For best results, remove the greenish yellow flowers back to the base as they fade, taking some of the older, faded leaves at the same time. This encourages new growth and another flush of flower later in summer.

Buxus suffruticosa (zones 5–6) is a dwarf form of common box and normally used as an edging plant. If planted 15cm (6in) apart, these plants will slowly form a low, dense hedge up to 30x30cm (1x1ft) high. It is ideal to define areas or to create a pattern in a formal area such as a parterre. It requires trimming once a year in early summer after the danger of frost has passed. It can also be used for small topiary or as the structural plant in a container, window box or hanging basket. It is tolerant of dry conditions and poor soil but fertile soil will produce darker evergreen foliage. Feed in spring and early summer but avoid feeding in late summer as this will encourage soft new growth into autumn, which is susceptible to winter frosts. If needed in quantity, it is cheaper to buy it bare rooted during the dormant season.

Tightly clipped and spiky variegated holly, *Ilex* 'Argentea Marginata', provides solid structure to other softer planting.

A cloud of small white flowers is held high on the tall delicate stems of *Crambe cordifolia*.

A topiary yew, *Taxus baccata*, surrounded by *Pachysandra terminalis* and ferns, *Polystichum* 'Herrenhausen' and a splash of white provided by *Euonymus* 'Emerald Gaiety'.

Ilex aquifolium 'Argentea Marginata' (zones 6–8) is a variegated holly with dark green leaves heavily margined with white, giving an overall silvery appearance. It is a useful evergreen for structural effect and can be pruned to shape and to control overall size. If allowed to grow unchecked, it will slowly reach a size of 4x3m (12x10ft) However, it is often used in a pruned form either in a cone or domed shape. Hollies are very tough and will thrive in most well-drained soils, including poor soil. They will tolerate part shade and windy sites. Look out for reversion; that is, plain green shoots that will overtake the variegated foliage. This should be removed immediately to avoid it spreading to other parts of the plant.

Crambe cordifolia (zones 5–8) is a large-growing perennial plant with enormous rounded leaves and large stems that are branched and covered with masses of small gypsophila-like white flowers during midsummer. The ends of the branched stems holding the flowers are delicate and from a distance the flowers appear as a cloud, unsupported. The usual height is 1.2–1.5m (4–5ft) but occasionally it grows up to 2.1m (7ft). It requires full sun and a moist well-drained site. The flowers react dramatically to drying out by dropping immediately. In exposed positions the stems may require staking, so sheltered situations are best. Look out for caterpillar damage. Crambe is part of the cabbage family and the leaves can be stripped down to the veins by caterpillars in a very short time.

Taxus baccata (zones 5–7) is the English yew that grows to a great age as a specimen and is widely used for hedging, screening or as clipped evergreen structure. If left to grow, it reaches an average size of 6m (20ft) high and wide, though very old trees are taller. It responds well to clipping, so it is popular for hedges and topiary, with dark green leaves on dense branches providing an excellent backdrop or framework for more short-term, showy planting. It is very useful in areas of the garden that require a strong planting structure of a density to complement strong building lines. Topiary and hedges, if repeated, also act to link areas of the garden, and yew is a larger, slightly coarser and darker alternative to box. It will thrive in sun or part shade and most soils but waterlogging means certain death.

TRADITIONAL TERRACE GARDEN

This garden includes the front and rear of a traditional house in the country. To the front, the garden provides a welcome entrance to the house, looking good all year round. It separates the car parking area from the house and is in shade for most of the day. The larger part of the garden is to the rear and is used mainly during the summer months as an outdoor family living room, leading directly from the kitchen and dining area. The terrace also functions as a link to the rest of the garden, which consists of sweeping lawns, established trees and shrubs and paddock surrounded by countryside. In full sun almost all day, it was necessary to introduce some shade element. The design and materials used for the garden blend with the period, rural style of the property, which is clad in old clay tiles and has many visible oak timbers.

PLANNING the GARDEN

Most gardens, particularly the areas adjacent to the house, are used as an extension to the home, and the family in this old manor house wanted a comfortable seating space just outside the family kitchen doors. What was required was a simple layout in a traditional style that would also link other parts of the garden. It should aim to create a feeling of privacy and cosiness without being cut off from the rest of the garden. As well as providing an area in which to sit, the terrace had to be designed to provide vistas to other parts of the garden and easy access from the various doors in the house.

So this is where the planning started: first laying out paths in various directions to fulfil the practical requirements and then mapping out the shape of the terrace to create an interesting shape, large enough to be practical and yet small enough to avoid a large expanse of harsh paving. A key part of the design is to provide plenty of space for planting between the house and the paving and large enough beds for bold planting in scale with the hard surfaces.

There was very little existing planting and the original paving, laid on sand, consisted of pieces of broken York stone. A low brick wall jutting out from the house was retained to maintain a sense of privacy by the back doors and to provide an excellent backdrop for a water feature.

Maintenance was not of great concern as a skilled gardener was available to maintain the planting. Nevertheless, it was decided to avoid plants that require specific staking or supporting. The garden is close to the house so it was necessary to ensure year-round interest and create a good strong planting framework in keeping with the solid appearance of the property and garden.

The soil here is very heavy clay with a reasonable topsoil above. Large cracks open up during dry summer months and it is prone to waterlogging in winter, so the ground preparation was, as ever, crucial to ensure the success of any planting.

The aspect is sunny and fairly sheltered by the house so it was necessary to create a degree of shade to sit under during the summer. Careful positioning of a pergola was decided upon to achieve a shady dining area away from the doors and without blocking important views of the rest of the garden.

The old brick pavers and old York stone join where the terrace and pathway meet. The greens, pinks and mauves of salvia, alchemilla, lavender and nepeta combine to blend with the terracotta tones of the old brick.

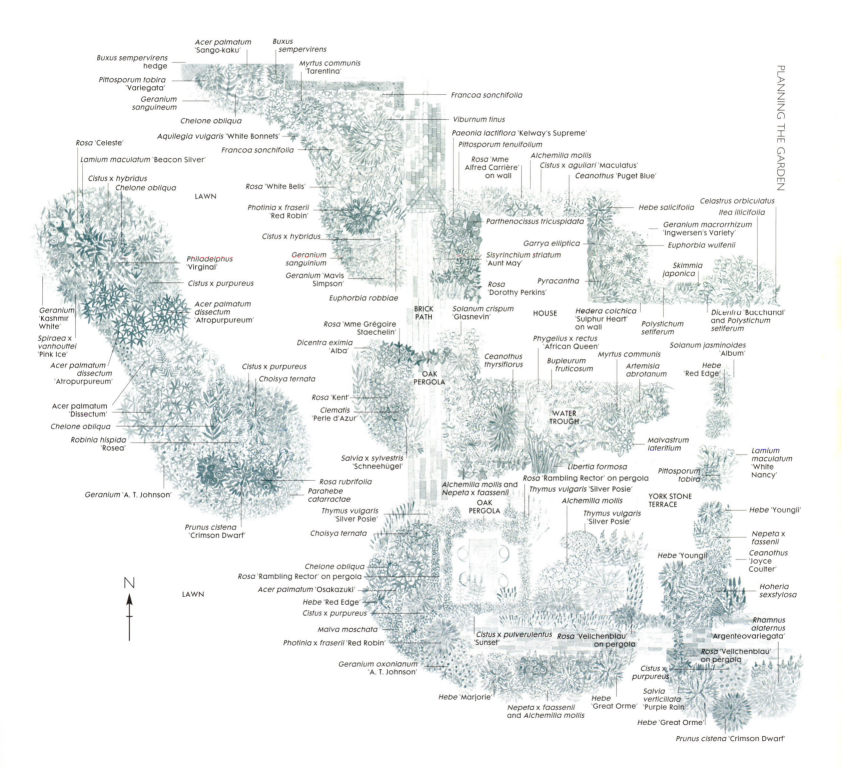

Buxus sempervirens hedge

Pittosporum tobira 'Variegata'

Geranium sanguineum

Acer palmatum 'Sango-kaku'

Buxus sempervirens

Myrtus communis 'Tarentina'

Chelone obliqua

Francoa sonchifolia

Viburnum tinus

Rosa 'Celeste'

Aquilegia vulgaris 'White Bonnets'

Paeonia lactiflora 'Kelway's Supreme'

Pittosporum tenuifolium

Lamium maculatum 'Beacon Silver'

Francoa sonchifolia

Rosa 'Mme Alfred Carrière' on wall

Alchemilla mollis

Cistus x aguilari 'Maculatus'

Cistus x hybridus

Chelone obliqua

Rosa 'White Bells'

Ceanothus 'Puget Blue'

LAWN

Photinia x fraserii 'Red Robin'

Hebe salicifolia

Celastrus orbiculatus

Itea illicifolia

Cistus x hybridus

Parthenocissus tricuspidata

Geranium macrorrhizum 'Ingwersen's Variety'

Philadelphus 'Virginal'

Geranium sanguinium

Garrya elliptica

Euphorbia wulfenii

Cistus x purpureus

Geranium 'Mavis Simpson'

Sisyrinchium striatum 'Aunt May'

Skimmia japonica

Euphorbia robbiae

Rosa 'Dorothy Perkins'

Pyracantha

Geranium 'Kashmir White'

Acer palmatum dissectum 'Atropurpureum'

BRICK PATH

Solanum crispum 'Glasnevin'

HOUSE

Hedera colchica 'Sulphur Heart' on wall

Dicentra 'Bacchanal' and Polystichum setiferum

Spiraea x vanhouttei 'Pink Ice'

Rosa 'Mme Grégoire Staechelin'

Polystichum setiferum

Acer palmatum dissectum 'Atropurpureum'

Dicentra eximia 'Alba'

Phygelius x rectus 'African Queen'

Solanum jasminoides 'Album'

Ceanothus thyrsiflorus

Bupleurum fruticosum

Myrtus communis

Artemisia abrotanum

Hebe 'Red Edge'

Acer palmatum 'Dissectum'

OAK PERGOLA

Chelone obliqua

Rosa 'Kent'

Robinia hispida 'Rosea'

Clematis 'Perle d'Azur'

WATER TROUGH

Malvastrum lateritium

Lamium maculatum 'White Nancy'

Cistus x purpureus

Choisya ternata

Libertia formosa

Pittosporum tobira

Salvia x sylvestris 'Schneehügel'

Rosa 'Rambling Rector' on pergola

Thymus vulgaris 'Silver Posie'

YORK STONE TERRACE

Geranium 'A. T. Johnson'

Rosa rubrifolia

Parahebe catarractae

Alchemilla mollis and Nepeta x faassenii

Alchemilla mollis

Hebe 'Youngii'

Thymus vulgaris 'Silver Posie'

OAK PERGOLA

Thymus vulgaris 'Silver Posie'

Nepeta x faassenii

Prunus cistena 'Crimson Dwarf'

Choisya ternata

Hebe 'Youngii'

Ceanothus 'Joyce Coulter'

N

Chelone obliqua

Rosa 'Rambling Rector' on pergola

Acer palmatum 'Osakazuki'

Hoheria sexstylosa

LAWN

Hebe 'Red Edge'

Cistus x purpureus

Malva moschata

Rhamnus alaternus 'Argenteovariegata'

Photinia x fraserii 'Red Robin'

Cistus x pulverulentus 'Sunset'

Rosa 'Veilchenblau' on pergola

Rosa 'Veilchenblau' on pergola

Geranium oxonianum 'A. T. Johnson'

Cistus x purpureus

Salvia verticillata 'Purple Rain'

Hebe 'Marjorie'

Nepeta x faassenii and Alchemilla mollis

Hebe 'Great Orme'

Hebe 'Great Orme'

Prunus cistena 'Crimson Dwarf'

SPECIAL FEATURES

All the components in this garden had to be solid and traditional, in keeping with the overall features of the property. The old York stone terrace is no exception. Random rectangular reclaimed York stone paving is one of the more expensive surfaces but has a wonderful weathered appearance and blends easily with an older house. Various grades are normally available, with the most expensive tending to be of uniform thickness, 5–7cm (2–3in), and varying in colour from dark blue-purple hues to greys and brown. It is a more challenging material to lay than concrete paving, especially when the individual slabs vary in thickness and are awkward and heavy to handle. For the most pleasing appearance it is best to dress the newly cut edges rather than leave a sharp-angled edge. As well as high cost, another disadvantage of this type of paving is that it can become slippery when wet. It is best avoided in shady areas where lichen and algae can exacerbate the problem. For better grip, old York paving is sometimes offered with a sandblasted surface. I always avoid supplies that have been sandblasted because the process can mask the presence of oil in the paving slab. Oil can occasionally be found in York stone where the slabs have been reclaimed from an old mill upon which machinery has stood for many years. Once the oil has impregnated the stone it is impossible to shift, and will normally only become apparent after the first shower of rain, creating unsightly oily stains.

This type of paving is becoming more difficult to obtain and hence more expensive. There is a variety of alternatives on the market. However, for this garden it was necessary to use the authentic York stone to match up with the existing slabs in various parts of the garden, including the doorsteps.

From the terrace there are two pathways linking the rest of the garden. Victorian brick pavers were used to continue the theme of old materials. They are thinner than the normal house brick with a worn surface and an attractive dark red often slightly mottled with black specks. The worn appearance rests easily with the old natural York stone. To construct these pathways, first two parallel edges of bricks placed end to end were cemented on an ample ridge of concrete for both sides of the path and allowed to set. Sharp sand was spread in the space between the bricks and the rest of the path infilled in a traditional bond with the brick surface set approximately 1cm (½in) above the sides already

Random rectangular York paving provides a neutral-coloured surface that looks as if it has been laid for years.

A shady dining area created by the oak pergola, clad with *Rosa* 'Rambling Rector'. Structural evergreen shrubs are *Photinia* 'Red Robin' (left) and *Pittosporum* 'Silver Queen' (right).

cemented. A vibrating plate was then run over the surface to bed them down to the same level as the sides, forcing some of the sharp sand between each brick to bond the whole pathway tightly. This creates a very firm, yet flexible, surface. Hard bricks should always be used as softer ones may break with the pressure from the vibrating plate.

Timber pergola

A major function of the terrace is to provide space to sit outside and use as a family dining area. A good, solid, timbered pergola was necessary to span an area over the table and chairs to provide dappled shade once the roses and clematis have established themselves on it. This pergola is made in green oak from 10x12.5cm (4x5in) timbers assembled using oak dowel pegs in the same manner that traditional timbered buildings were constructed years ago. The appearance is very much in keeping with the old manor house and the solid feel fits with the heavy features, such as the York and brick paving. The span is approximately 2.5m (8ft) square, providing room for the large stone-topped dining table with wrought-iron base. Head clearance under the pergola should be at least 2.1m (6ft10in), and with this size of timber I do not recommend a span of more than 3m (10ft) without additional uprights. The larger the span of pergola, the higher the pergola should be to maintain correct proportions. It is also important to allow enough space for plants growing on the pergola to hang down, while still allowing people to walk freely underneath.

As the planting develops, wires can be fixed across the span of timber to train the climbers for a dense canopy. In this case the top was left open as sufficient shade was cast by the vigorous roses tied to the overhead timbers. The posts are set approximately 60cm (2ft) into the ground and this solid construction should last for many years. I do not advise cementing in the posts unless they are unsupported. Far better to allow the pergola to move with the heave of the ground as it shifts with the ever-changing moisture content.

When assembled, the oak timbers are normally very light in colour and exude a dark brown liquid during the first showers of rain that stain anything underneath them, including paving. This is the tannin in the oak timber that will eventually fade even on light-coloured surfaces. The timber gradually turns to a honey colour before weathering to an attractive silver grey, as they have now in this garden. It is not necessary to oil the timbers, although in some cases this is carried out to retain a lighter colour.

To balance the terrace pergola, two small sections of oak pergola built in the

A carved York stone-topped table in the dining area gives a sense of permanence and continuity with the York stone-paved terrace.

same style are positioned in an 'L' shape over the brick pathways that lead to either side of the house. These pergolas continue the height away from the main terrace while still allowing views of the garden beyond and help to create a cosy, intimate atmosphere as each section forms a window through which different parts of the garden can be viewed.

Water spout

The existing wall, built at right angles to the house and partially covered by a large ceanothus on one side, was used to mount a water spout. It is fed by pipework on the other side, flowing into an old galvanized cattle trough to produce the sound of running water and is surrounded by water plants. The water is circulated by means of a small submersible pump tucked away at one end of the trough and covered by planting. A slab of old York stone is placed in the surrounding bed to allow access to the trough with origanum flowing around the base of the trough and surrounding the paving slab.

PLANTS and PLANTING

The garden close to the house already had some established plants, as did the outer edges, and it was important to blend the newly introduced shrubs and perennials with existing planting. The ceanothus, for example, was well established and played a large part in softening the brick wall jutting out from the house. However, once the flowers are over in early summer there is a need for later colour and so small shrubs and perennials are drifted around the base. The pergolas, which play an important part in this garden both for shade and for dividing up the space, are planted with roses and clematis only, using three varieties of climbing or rambling rose to avoid a common mistake of too many varieties, which can result in a patchy appearance. If more than one variety of climber is used on a pergola or arch, use at least the same variety on uprights on opposite sides of a path for some continuity.

The aspect is quite open and windy, though the pergolas and established planting surrounding the garden provide a degree of wind filtration. As it is an old established garden, the topsoil is good loam though underneath is heavy clay. It was therefore poorly drained initially and some of the lavenders and catmint had to be replaced after the first winter, due to waterlogging. This was less of a problem in subsequent years when the soil had eventually settled down after the initial disturbance during construction and planting of the garden.

In the shade, *Polystichum setiferum* ferns flourish in a narrow bed surrounded by *Dicentra* 'Bacchanal'. In the background on the wall is a large-leafed variegated ivy, *Hedera colchica* 'Sulphur Heart'.

Polystichum setiferum (zones 6–8), the soft shield fern, is evergreen/semi-evergreen, thrives in moist shade and is very hardy. It is used here in a repetitive pattern because of the narrow bed. *Dicentra* 'Bacchanal' (zones 3–9), drifted around the base of the bed, is perhaps the darkest pink, almost ruby-red, variety. It thrives in semi-shade, moist well-drained conditions and flowers in late spring and early summer. The attractive light green ferny foliage dies back to ground level every winter. Slugs can be a problem as they eat the new shoots in spring. *Hedera colchica* 'Sulphur Heart' (zones 6–9) is a large-leafed ivy with splashes of lime-green variegation. It is ideal for shady conditions and will withstand poor soils though it resents excessively dry conditions. It is useful because its lime-green variegation is a good foil for other shade plants with white or blue flowers.

Scrambling up the timber cladding, the golden hop, *Humulus lupulus* 'Aureus', contrasts well with the bright blue flowers of *Ceanothus* 'Puget Blue'.

Humulus lupulus 'Aureus' (zones 3–8), the golden-leafed hop, is a very vigorous twining climber and the golden-leafed variation of the hop used for beer. The stems die back to ground level every year and will quickly reach heights of up to 6m (20ft) by midsummer, though not in the first year of planting. The roots need to be well established before this climber can become quite rampant, smothering sheds, pergolas or small trees. It is particularly useful to create temporary summer shade close to the house as, being herbaceous, it can be cleared completely in autumn, thus not blocking valuable winter light. By late summer small hop flowers will form and, grown with *Lonicera* x *heckrottii*, makes an attractive combination of lime green, cream and purple. Beware, as the stems are hairy and very rough and can cause a painful skin burn if drawn across the face.

Ceanothus thyrsiflorus smothers the end of the brick wall jutting out from the house. In the centre foreground *Libertia formosa* stands out with spiky leaves and clear white flowers.

The bright rosy pink heads of *Cistus* x *purpureus* flower all summer and create a pleasant screen around the seating area.

A brick path under a pergola of *Rosa* 'Mme Grégoire Staechelin', with the pinks of the paving echoed in the planting of *Paeonia lactiflora* 'Kelway's Supreme' (lower right).

Libertia formosa (zones 8–10), with spiky grass-like leaves, forms a wide clump up to 60cm (2ft) wide and 90cm (3ft) high. Libertia will survive in part shade but is better in full sun in a sheltered position with good drainage. Successful only in mild areas, it has pure white saucer-shaped flowers with yellow centres above the leaves. Unfortunately, older leaves can turn brown at the tips and these should be removed or trimmed with scissors to a point. It is an attractive, useful plant throughout the year, with bright green evergreen leaves and flowers that form orange seed pods in autumn. It has a finer leafed sister, *Libertia ixioides*, which has dark green leaves turning to an attractive bronze colour during winter. Libertia can be easily propagated by division in spring.

Cistus x *purpureus* (zones 7–10) grows to 1.5m (5ft) and is very useful as a structural plant. Each flower is quite short lived but it has a succession, throughout the summer, of rich pink, tissue paper thin petals with a dark red blotch. The leaves are narrow and evergreen and pruning is best carried out by thinning rather than trimming during the growing season, plus a light trim at the end of flowering in late summer. The soil must be well drained and the aspect sunny. Cistus do not demand high levels of nutrient and will even thrive on poor, thin soils.

Rosa 'Mme Grégoire Staechelin' (zones 5–9) grows to 6m (20ft) and, although used in a sunny position here, will also thrive on a north or east wall. The coral-pink flowers appear once for several weeks during midsummer. The flowers are strongly scented, rather blowsy and hang down from thorny stems. To extend the season of interest I have planted *Clematis* 'Perle d'Azur' twined through the rose. A combination of light blue and pink flowers clothing the pergola complement the blue and pink combination of perennials below and the clematis continues to flower after the rose has finished. *Paeonia lactiflora* 'Kelway's Supreme' (zones 3–8) has very fragrant soft pink double flowers from late spring until early summer and good autumn leaf colour. The soil should be rich and well drained in a sunny position.

The pale green leaves of *Acer palmatum* 'Sango-kaku' in the background are surrounded by the dark green leaves of the later flowering *Chelone obliqua*. Bottom right are *Aquilegia* 'Pink Bonnets' and 'Blue Bonnets' self-seeding to mingle with the rest of the planting.

Rosa 'Rambling Rector', almost at its peak of flowering, envelops the pergola and frames the windows in the background.

Acer palmatum 'Sango-kaku' (zones 5–8) has many varied attributes and, if one Japanese maple only could be grown, this would be a good contender. The new growth in spring is tinged bronze before turning light green through the summer. By autumn the leaves turn butter yellow before falling as a yellow carpet around this slender, elegant tree that grows up to 6m (20ft). For good autumn colour acers require plenty of light and some sun, though they can be prone to leaf scorch in high levels of sunshine. The most critical time for foliage is late spring just as the shoots are developing though just as the

shoots burst, when there is a danger of late frosts causing dieback. Later on look out for dead stems that can attract coral spot – small orange dots on dead wood that can spread to the live and should be removed immediately. When planting young Japanese maples the planting level is critical. Most plants will not tolerate their stems buried too deep. However, acers are particularly sensitive as they have very thin bark that will rot away if planting is too deep, resulting in the death of the tree.

Rosa 'Rambling Rector' (zones 5–9) is very similar to *Rosa* 'Seagull' and is equally vigorous, quickly reaching 6m (20ft) or more. During early midsummer it will become covered in large heads of small creamy white flowers. The scented flowers appear only once during the summer but, when they do, it is normally for at least three to four weeks and in very large quantity. If dead heads are not removed by autumn, small red fruits will form. Old stems should be removed each year and the previous season's growth tied in to carry the flowers early the following summer.

The small evergreen shrub *Daphne odora* 'Aureomarginata', with its dark green leaves, underplanted with *Rosmarinus prostratus*.

The large green globes of *Hydrangea arborescens* 'Annabelle' (right) combine well *with Ilex aquifolium* 'Argentea Marginata' (left) and *Hydrangea anomala petiolaris* against the wall.

Photinia 'Red Robin' forms a splash of deep red in the centre, while a drift of greenish yellow *Euphorbia amygdaloides robbiae* grows in the foreground and white *Viburnum opulus* 'Roseum' in the background.

Daphne odora 'Aureomarginata' (zones 7–9) is one of the most popular daphnes, probably because it is evergreen. The best conditions for this plant to succeed are a lightly shaded spot, away from the sun during the hottest part of the day and sheltered from wind, in moist, rich loamy soil yet very well drained. They have a brittle, fleshy root system, making them very difficult to transplant successfully. I have also had very limited success growing them in pots as they are sensitive to drying out or overwatering. Having made them sound very difficult, *Daphne odora* 'Aureomarginata' is well worth growing. If you find just the right position, the plant will absolutely thrive. It will have dark green leaves margined yellow and highly scented dark pink flowers during late winter and into early spring.

Hydrangea arborescens 'Annabelle' (zones 3–9) grows up to 1.5m (5ft) high and wide. Because it flowers during mid- to late summer, it is best cut back hard to 20cm (6–8in) above ground level in late winter. This allows for fresh new stems to develop the following summer on which are produced very large heads of flowers that start off green and slowly turn white. It is best grown in partial shade in moist soil, but not close to other shrubs or in windy situations. *Hydrangea anomala petiolaris* (zones 4–8) also requires moist soil and often lacks the moisture it needs due to overhanging roofs. It is however an ideal plant for a sunless wall and, although slow to establish, it will quickly climb to 10m (30ft) or more. It is self-clinging and so can do harm to tiled roofs, paintwork and gutters if left unchecked.

Euphorbia amygdaloides robbiae (zones 6–8) is an extremely useful plant for groundcover in shade or semi-shade. It thrives in almost any well-drained soil and will tolerate very dry conditions. With evergreen leaves that grow to 30cm (1ft) it has rounded heads of lime-green flowers above, giving it an overall height of 60cm (2ft) and a spread of 60–90cm (2–3ft). It may spread even further with its underground stems and can be quite invasive in small areas. I often use this plant in shade at the base of a fence where it should be planted about 60cm (2ft) apart for quick groundcover and used in drifts rather than singly. It looks good planted with other shade-tolerant plants such as variegated ivy, symphytum and lamium. Caution should be taken as all euphorbias have a poisonous milky sap that is also a skin and eye irritant.

SWIMMING POOL GARDEN

This pool area is situated well away from the house and includes a traditional barn-style pool building for changing, entertaining and storage. It is positioned on the edge of the main garden and surrounded by rolling countryside. It cannot rely on the house for structure and has to have its own surround without screening the adjoining land and far-reaching views. A shelter belt of fastigiate hornbeam together with the barn building provide a sturdy yet visually soft boundary on two sides. The other two sides have a more subtle enclosure of planting and pergola, allowing views of the rest of the garden and farmland beyond. The garden is intended to provide a space for relaxation and peace combined with the fun and excitement of the pool.

PLANNING the GARDEN

Positioned between the house and a tennis court, the swimming pool in this garden is the central feature and situated about 50m (165ft) from the house. The site was originally open field with a tennis court nearby the proposed pool and surrounded by farmland.

In addition to the area immediately around the pool, it was necessary to incorporate new pathways linking the new garden with the tennis court and the house. At the opposite end of the new pool a traditional barn-style pool house was designed for storage and changing rooms. The ground sloped gently down towards the tennis court and so we had to level the area for the pool and surrounding paving so that changes in level could be subtly incorporated into the planted areas. It would not be practical or safe to have steps. Large quantities of topsoil were graded around the pool surround to blend the levels gently.

Behind the pool house a small shed housing the pool equipment had to be hidden away from view. What was required was plenty of open space for a large family to enjoy the pool and its surrounding area. Swimming pools tend to attract large numbers of children and therefore it was important to provide clear, safe access with features and seating areas well away from the pool surround. For pools such as this one situated away from the house and mainly used during the summer, it is possible to concentrate on summer season interest with the plants rather than year-round planting but it still needed a good basic planting structure. Evergreen planting here is less important than lots of summer colour.

The balance and scale of each element required careful consideration as the pool and pool building are on such a large scale. The beds therefore had to be generous in size to accommodate bold planting. There were a number of existing plants to incorporate into the design and some mature trees on the edge of the site.

Far-reaching views had to be considered from the southern end of the garden and a small rectangular area of paving was planned in the south-east corner of the swimming pool surround for a small table and chairs.

The pool area is part of a larger garden and there was concern that it should not become too dominant. It was a challenge, therefore, to keep the swimming pool obscured from other parts of the garden while maintaining the open views from the pool and at the same time provide a private atmosphere around the pool and its immediate surroundings.

The soil conditions are very heavy clay that was badly compacted by machinery during the pool construction, so as soon as the soil dried out sufficiently we had to use a sub-soiling machine to loosen up the soil and ease the compaction before any planting could be carried out.

A swathe of *Nepeta x faassenii* and *Knautia macedonica* carpet the ground surrounding the garden bench.

Acer negundo 'Flamingo'

Geranium thurstonianum

HORNBEAM SHELTER

Geranium x cantabrigiense 'Biokovo'
GATE

Mixed country hedge

WILDFLOWER MEADOW

Elaeagnus x ebbingei

Geranium phaeum

Euonymus fortunei 'Emerald Gaiety'

Photinia 'Red Robin'

Carpinus betulus 'Fastigiata'

PUMP SHED

Rosa 'New Dawn' on pergola

Geranium x oxonianum 'A. T. Johnson'

Pittisporum tenuifolium

POOL HOUSE

Carpinus betulus 'Fastigiata'

Cistus x purpureus

Escallonia 'Apple Blossom'

Hebe 'Great Orme'

Rosa 'Charles de Mills'

Rosa 'De Rescht'

BARK PATH

Jasminium officinale

Sisyrinchium striatum 'Aunt May'

Cistus 'Grayswood Pink'

Rosa 'François Juranville' on pergola

Hebe 'Marjorie'

Acer brilliantissimum

Origanum vulgare 'Aureum'

Geranium sanguineum

Hebe 'Great Orme'

Cistus x purpureus

Alchemilla mollis

Lavandula angustifolia

Buddleja davidii 'Black Knight'

Hebe 'Wiri Cloud'

Rosa rugosa 'Alba', Rosa 'Scabrosa' and Rosa 'Agnes'

Rosa 'François Juranville' on pergola

Geranium sanguineum 'Striatum'

Geranium thurstonianum

Geranium wlassovianum

Spiraea japonica 'Gold Mound'

GRASS PATH

Prunus padus 'Watereri'

Prunus cerasifera 'Pissardii'

TERRACE INDIAN SANDSTONE

Geranium sanguineum

Catalpa bignonioides 'Aurea'

Agapanthus 'Headbourne Hybrids'

Geranium renardii

BRICK EDGE

Hebe salicifolia

CRETAN URN water feature

POOL

Weigela florida 'Variegata'

Hemerocallis fulva 'Plena'

Ceanothus 'Joyce Coulter'

Choisya ternata 'Sundance'

Knautia macedonica

Phygelius x rectus 'African Queen'

Rosa 'Blairii Number Two' on pergola

Rosa 'Blairii Number Two' on pergola

Knautia macedonica

Phlomis fruticosa

Artemisia abrotanum

Geranium renardii

Nepeta 'Walker's Low'

Philadelphus 'Virginal'

Rosa 'Prosperity'

Spiraea japonica 'Goldflame'

Lavandula pedunculata

SEATING AREA

Malus 'John Downie' tree

Rosa 'Leverkusen' and Clematis 'Mme Julia Correvon' on pergola

Geranium wlassovianum and Verbena bonariensis

Physocarpus opulifolius 'Luteus'

Knautia macedonica

Sorbus vilmorinii

Teucrium fruticans

Perovskia 'Blue Spire'

Cercis canadensis 'Forest Pansy'

Potentilla 'Tangerine'

Malva moschata rosea

Geranium wlassovianum

Hebe 'Youngii'

TO THE HOUSE

Hebe 'Autumn Glory' and Lavandula stoechas 'Snowman'

Lavandula 'Vera'

Geum rivale 'Leonard's Variety'

N

Kniphofia galpinii

Ceratostigma griffithii

BRICK PATH

Geranium sanguineum 'Max Frei'

Cistus x purpureus

Hebe 'Mrs Winder'

Views

Buddleja 'Black Knight'

Cistus x purpureus

SPECIAL FEATURES

Most swimming pools require a building for storage, changing and to house the pool treatment plant. In this case a large oak-framed barn-style building clad with feather-edged timber and a traditional clay tile roof also incorporates space to sit in comfort, sheltered from wind and rain. The paving surrounding the pool continues into the building, creating a link between the inside and outside.

Paving

Surrounding the pool is an area of paving to provide ample space for sitting, playing and accessing the pool. To create space for several tables and numerous chairs for a large family to enjoy the pool and its surroundings all day long, a large paved area is necessary. It is

The seating area is positioned a short distance from the poolside for views across the garden and surrounded by planting.

tempting, therefore, simply to put a vast area of paving right around the pool and this is often done. Inevitably, the result can be stark and utilitarian in appearance and atmosphere, particularly during the winter months when the pool is not in use.

A better solution is to plan the space for visual as well as practical purposes and, in this case, a brick path was designed round the whole pool, wider than normal for safety and to keep the plants a reasonable distance from splashes of chlorinated water. Then, where seating was needed, the path was widened considerably in a stepped shape to provide lots of space softened at the edges by planting. This gives the effect of a number of linked individual spaces to accommodate one small table and chair for a small group or several large tables and many chairs.

A winding brick path with planting flowing over the edges.

To appreciate the views across open countryside, the pool surround opens out into an area approximately 2x3m (6½x10ft) on the north-west corner for a small table and chairs. It is also an ideal spot to enjoy the late evening sun.

The paving surrounding the pool is Indian sandstone, which has become popular in recent years. It has the advantage of being cheaper than reclaimed rectangular York stone and is supplied in uniform thickness. The surface has enough texture to help reduce the danger of slipping, especially important when used around a swimming pool, where it will regularly be sprayed with water and a simple trip or slip could prove serious. The edges must be smooth and the join between the bevelled edge of the pool and paving slabs laid evenly to avoid damage to bare feet.

Water feature

Positioned away from the pool and building is the water feature. This provides the gentle sound and movement of running water and also acts as an introduction to the swimming pool area. The water feature is situated by the main grass pathway and forms a focal point through planting when viewed from the house. This has the effect of reducing the otherwise dominant presence of the swimming pool. To construct this water feature, we had to dig a square hole that was approximately 1.5x1.5m (5x5ft) and 90cm (3ft) deep, then line the hole with a butyl pond liner 3.5m (11½ft) square. It is important to ensure a protective layer of matting lines the hole to prevent any stones from perforating the liner. Concrete was then poured on top to form a base 30cm (1ft) thick in the bottom of the hole and left to set.

When the concrete was set firmly, a wall was constructed all the way round the hole, close to the edge of the liner to within one layer of bricks from the top. Bricks were then laid in the base and the top was capped off with small, half bull-nose header bricks on edge. A duct in the form of a piece of flexible pipe needed to be installed while this wall was being constructed, to carry an electric cable for the water pump later on. This duct had to run from the bottom of the hole, through the brickwork and up to the top between the bricks and the liner. In the centre of the brick-lined hole a plinth was constructed approximately 40cm (1½ft) square that was finished just below the level of the second course of brickwork in the wall. This plinth is hollow to house the submersible pump and should have an opening on one side to install and access the pump.

The main feature, a Cretan urn, was now placed on top of the plinth with a hole drilled in the bottom and a rigid pipe glued into it. The pipe should be fitted to just below the top rim of the pot and protrude below the base. A small submersible pump was then attached to the bottom of the pipe and connected to an electricity supply. When the pond and the pot are full of water, the pump circulates the water, creating a cascade down the ribbed sides of the pot, rippling into the water below.

The reservoir of water must be wide enough to contain the water as it splashes down from the pot and allow for the wind to spread the water even farther so that the water level does not have to be topped up too frequently. The pot supplier may supply the pot already drilled at the base with the pipe attached.

Although these Cretan pots are recommended for leaving out all year round, it would be advisable to drain the pot and, if possible, store it in a frost-free place during winter.

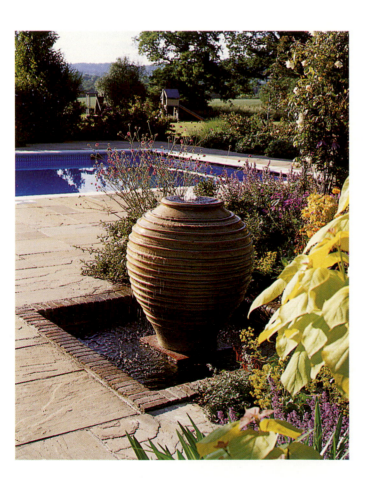

With planting on two sides of this water feature it was not necessary to use any water plants, which could have looked fussy. It may be necessary to treat the water with an algicide to prevent it from turning green but, if you have pets, ensure that it is safe for them to drink as this water feature is often known to double as a drinking trough.

Between the beds on the south side a meandering grass path leads to a wildflower meadow via a gate at one side of the pool building and a pergola designed in a curved shape is planted with rambling roses and clematis.

Hornbeam shelter

Between the pool building and pergola is a living hornbeam shelter. It is no more than 2m (6½ft) in diameter with a gap in the front looking out over the garden. This provides a quiet place to sit in the shade away from the noise and fun of the swimming pool. It has been created by planting 2m (6½ft) high, branched, hornbeam trees in a circle, pulling the tops together and tying them

An urn from Crete has been converted into a water feature standing in a brick-edged sump. Indian sandstone paving is laid on two sides with *Alchemilla mollis* and *Geranium clarkei* 'Kashmir Purple' flowing over the edge.

The rose-covered pergola provides a background for a seating area.

in to form an igloo shape. When they have grown together all that is necessary is to keep them trimmed twice every year. The base and the path leading from the lawn are laid with chipped bark, which is less formal and more practical than grass.

Pergola

To create a subtle barrier between the pool and the rest of the garden and to shield the pool from the house, a series of oak pergolas is positioned across the grass path. Pergolas used in this way provide defined spaces, one leading into the next with views through the various 'windows' created by them. These windows are most effective when the colour and texture from the climbers used on the pergola are reflected in the planting underneath.

PLANTS and PLANTING

The planting in this garden has to be bold to remain in proportion with the large areas of paving and the pool. This is achieved by using a strong framework planting, including the fastigiate hornbeam and large-growing roses plus some carefully positioned colourful trees such as *Prunus cerasifera* 'Nigra', *Catalpa bignonioides* 'Aurea', *Acer pseudoplatanus* 'Brilliantissimum', *Acer negundo* 'Flamingo' and *Sorbus hupehensis*. Ground conditions here are clay loam over heavy clay and the garden is in full sun all day.

The garden is designed to be used mainly through the summer months so the planting can be concentrated for this season, perhaps more than in most gardens. Plants are used in large drifts, keeping mainly to rugosa roses and *Geranium sanguineum* in front of the hornbeam. On the opposite side of the garden, the planting is rather more fussy, with shrubs and perennials chosen to complement the roses and clematis on the pergolas and attention is given to softening the edges of the paved pool terrace using sisyrinchium, nepeta, prostrate ceanothus, knautia and golden origanum. Flower and leaf colour on the pergolas and in large shrubs are reflected lower down to ensure unity and continuity. Thus the golden catalpa has a patch of golden origanum close by with a contrasting plant, in this case agapanthus, in between. Drifts of potentilla soften the edges of brick paths and the stunning and architectural, spiky form of kniphofia creates a focal point on the open side of the garden.

Carpinus betulus 'Fastigiata' (fastigiate hornbeam) forms a 'rolling' backdrop for the swimming pool garden. A drift of rugosa roses fronted with *Geranium sanguineum* forms easily maintained summer planting.

Potentilla fruticosa 'Tangerine' flows over the edge of a winding brick path.

Rosa rugosa (zones 2–7) come in a wide range of varieties. There are several used here, including *Rosa rugosa* 'Agnes', *R. r.* 'Scabrosa' and *R. r.* 'Alba'. Of these, *R. r.* 'Agnes' is perhaps the least common, with very scented, pale creamy yellow flowers during early summer and a few later on. It is vigorous, growing to 2.4x2.4m (8x8ft), with thorny stems. *R. r.* 'Scabrosa' and *R. r.* 'Alba' are slightly smaller, up to 2x2m (6½x6½ft). 'Alba' has white flowers and 'Scabrosa', which flowers all summer, has larger, purplish pink flowers. All require plenty of sun for maximum flowering and prefer rich loamy soil, but equally they thrive on heavy clay or thin stony ground provided they do not dry out for long periods. *Rosa rugosa* varieties have large, attractive hips during late summer and autumn, so pruning is best done by removal of old branches in spring.

Potentilla fruticosa '**Tangerine**' (zones 2–7) is a popular variety that I find useful as a transition from bright colours to softer shades. It has tangerine or pale orange-coloured flowers and grows to 1.2x1.5m (4x5ft). The pale green leaves are a good foil for the flowers and it can be used to tone down bright yellow varieties such as *Potentilla* 'Goldfinger'. Best planted in drifts or repetitively rather than just the odd one here and there, potentillas are deciduous and therefore rather boring in winter. In a garden requiring year-round interest, they require evergreen companions such as *Artemisia* 'Powis Castle', hebe or cistus for winter interest. Potentillas will thrive in most soils except poorly drained and require hard pruning by trimming in late winter.

The golden yellow foliage of *Physocarpus opulifolius* 'Luteus' stands out against a dark background.

Rosa 'François Juranville' (top centre) smothers the front pergola with soft pink flowers and to the left is the slightly deeper pink climbing *Rosa* 'Constance Spry'. *Rosa* 'Charles de Mills' can be seen front right, with *Rosa* 'De Rescht' to the right and *Cistus* x *purpureus* in between.

Physocarpus opulifolius '**Luteus**' (zones 2–7) grows to 2x2m (6½x6½ft). With bright yellow leaves and white flowers presented in early summer, this deciduous shrub will draw the attention and brighten dull areas of the garden. It is useful for contrasts and when planted with dark purple foliage such as *Cotinus* 'Royal Purple', *Sambucus* 'Black Beauty' or *Prunus cerasifera* 'Nigra' provides a dramatic effect. However, if planted in light shade, the bright yellow leaves turn lime green, opening up another range of planting partners such as the fresh green-leafed groundcover of *Pachysandra terminalis*, *Tiarella cordifolia* or *Geranium sanguineum* 'Album'. Physocarpus should be pruned in the same way as deutzias and philadelphus (see page 136). It requires moist acid soil and little maintenance.

For the ultimate in fragrant and frothy pink and purple roses during early to midsummer the following take some beating. All are once flowering, though occasional flowers can appear later in the season. *Rosa* '**François Juranville**' (zones 5–7) has large, scented, light apricot-pink double flowers with an attractive old-fashioned style. The advantage of once-flowering climbers and ramblers is the abundance of flower at one time, lasting for up to six weeks, and this variety is no exception. It will grow up to 6m (20ft) with long glossy green shoots. It is prone to mildew so keep it well watered during dry periods. *Rosa* '**Constance Spry**' (zones 5–7) is a shrub or climbing rose with highly scented large pale pink flowers. The stems are covered with many, fine red thorns.

The scent alone makes it well worth growing. Gallica shrub rose *Rosa* '**Charles de Mills**' (zones 5–7) has flat dark crimson-purple flowers that are highly scented and quartered. With upright growth up to 1.5m (5ft), the branches are arching and dark green. *Rosa* '**De Rescht**' (zones 5–7) will eventually reach 1.8m (6ft) but can easily be kept to 1.2m (4ft). It has richly scented, double, rosette-shaped rich pink flowers. This variety of damask rose sometimes flowers several times in late summer to autumn. To encourage more flowering and sturdy plants, dead heads can be removed by pruning the flower stem back to within two buds of the main stem. This will also encourage fresh new growth to develop ready for flowering the next year.

Knautia macedonica flowers flop over the edge of the sandstone paving, providing flowers throughout the summer months.

Deep purplish pink *Lavandula stoechas* 'Pedunculata' softens the edge of the paving.

Kniphofia galpinii, or red hot pokers, provide a succession of flowers during late summer and autumn.

Knautia macedonica (zones 5–9), also known as *Scabiosa rumelica,* is a member of the scabious family, enjoying recent popularity. It requires a sunny, well-drained position and will thrive on poor, dry sites. If the foliage is affected by mildew, keep the roots moist and it should grow out of the problem. The leaves form a rosette at the base with tall spikes up to 80cm (2½ft) on which round, double, dark crimson red flowers form. Even the new buds and dead heads are attractive and the flowers appear continuously during early to midsummer. Often, by late summer, the plant dies back and new leaves appear at the base. If the old spikes are removed, there may be time for a further flush of flower into autumn. If grown close to woody plants that will support the lax stems, this is preferable to staking.

Lavandula stoechas 'Pedunculata' (zones 6–9) is often referred to as *Lavandula* 'Papillon' and is a form of French lavender. It has deep purple flowers on globular heads with pale pink feather-like bracts above the flowerheads. The habit is more upright than *Lavandula stoechas* and it tends to flower earlier, often by early summer with another flush of flower during midsummer. The foliage is very aromatic and silvery green. Reaching a height and spread of 60x45cm (24x18in), the plants should be trimmed immediately after flowering to ensure a bushy habit. Like all lavenders, drainage must be good and the site should be in full sun. French lavenders are less hardy than the English or Dutch types and if at first they do not overwinter, either try the hardier angustifolia types or be resigned to replacing them with new ones each year.

Kniphofia galpinii (zones 4–9), also known as *Kniphofia triangularis,* is the traditional red hot poker. It requires full sun, rich well-drained soil and must be kept moist during the summer months. The leaves are narrow, grass-like and form a graceful tuft through which the tall flower spikes emerge up to 1m (3ft) high during late summer to give the appearance of fireworks. While orange is not my favourite colour in the garden, these flowers have great architectural appeal and appear at a time in summer when colours begin to wane. This variety is very hardy and can be propagated by seed or division in spring. For more subtle colours, try *Kniphofia* 'Percy's Pride' (zones 4–9) with tall lime-green/cream flowers or *Kniphofia* 'Little Maid' (zone 5) with shorter 60cm (2ft) creamy yellow flowers.

Rosa 'Leverkusen' climbs over the pergola, with *Clematis viticella* 'Mme Julia Correvon' giving a mass of flowers in late summer.

The tall fluffy spikes of pale blue *Nepeta racemosa* 'Walker's Low' can be seen in the foreground and *Lavandula stoechas* 'Pedunculata' in the background. Flowing between the two is *Geranium sanguineum*.

The pollarded *Catalpa bignonioides* 'Aurea' provides a lime-green background to the water feature with contrasting orange-red *Phygelius* 'African Queen'.

Rosa **'Leverkusen'** (zones 5–7) is a climbing rose I use for its very pale yellow, almost creamy flowers in clusters on a background of fresh light green leaves. The flowers are large and sweetly scented, appearing in a main flush during early summer with sporadic blooms later on. Ultimate height is 3m (10ft), so it is not too unruly on this pergola and pruning and training is quite simple with replacement of some old shoots and regular tying in. To keep free of mildew and black spot, water regularly during dry periods.
Clematis viticella **'Mme Julia Correvon'** (zones 4–9) does not suffer from wilt and begins flowering in midsummer, continuing right through to early autumn with masses of bright red flowers with golden stamens. All the viticella clematis require pruning down to 60–80cm (2–2½ft) in early spring.

Nepeta racemosa **'Walker's Low'** (zones 4–8) takes some beating for continuous summer flower and versatility. As a taller variety of catmint or catnip, growing 45–60cm (18–24in) high, the bluish purple flowers are rather more intense than the commonly grown *Nepeta* 'Six Hills Giant'. To encourage fresh new growth and maximum flowering, trim back old flowers regularly throughout the summer. Once established, nepeta will withstand drought but is prone to rotting off in wet soils over winter. It can be used to good effect between shrub roses; the mauve flowers associate well with pink, yellow or white roses and intersperse attractively with lime greens such as *Alchemilla mollis* and the silver foliage of *Artemisia* 'Lambrook Silver'. Propagation is easy by division into three or four plants in early spring.

Phygelius x *rectus* **'African Queen'** (zones 7–9) has orange-red tubular flowers from midsummer until early autumn. Reaching a height of 11m (3ft) and a width of 1.2m (4ft), it requires full sun or light shade and good drainage. In mild areas it can be grown as a shrub with a combination of growth from the base and from old wood. In colder positions it is cut to the ground over winter by frosts and will re-grow from the base. To induce more growth from the base, cut back to half in late spring and then older wood to the ground later on. It is, therefore, considered an evergreen or semi-evergreen shrub. In this garden, the strong colour is used to dramatic effect with the lime-green leaves of a pollarded *Catalpa bignonioides* 'Aurea'.

DRIVEWAY AND FRONT GARDEN

This suburban front garden has a gravel drive through the middle and spaces for car parking. The planting is in wide beds and the focal point is the front door, with a welcoming brick path echoed on the opposite side of the drive in a seating area. As a front garden it has to look good all year round and this is achieved by a good evergreen structure close to the house and a wide range of planting to provide continuing interest. The planting is banked on either side of the drive with deep drifts of plants indented on each side with brick paving or lawn, exaggerating the width of the space in front of the house.

PLANNING the GARDEN

Originally this drive led right up to the front door with a narrow strip of grass and trees on the opposite side. The challenge in planning here was to provide plenty of space for parking and easy access while, with the use of design and planting, reducing the visual impact on the garden of parked cars in the drive.

It was also necessary to allow space for several cars, leaving room for passing in the drive and for doors to open without crushing plants or walking on the beds. Sharp corners were avoided and flowing curves make the space more accessible. Space had to be created for planting to soften the impact of parked cars on the garden.

The owners wanted the house to be visually separated from the drive with a wide swathe of planting. This also extended the approach to the front door, making it appear more welcoming than in the original layout. A wide, generous path of brick was laid to emphasize the approach and was

Deep beds with bold drifts of fresh green and blue planting separate the house from the drive.

continued on the opposite side of the drive to create a new seating area that further reduced the impact of the drive on the entrance to the house.

The driveway has a sunny aspect and the soil is light, stony and well drained. This allows a wide range of plants to be used but plenty of organic matter had to be dug in to increase nutrients and moisture retention.

At one end of the drive is a steep slope leading to the garage and this required a stable surface rather than loose gravel. Fine gravel rolled into tarmac was chosen to retain a soft appearance with a brick standing area in front of the garage.

To one side of the house is access to the rear garden. This required a path via a gate leading from the drive with a layout and planting that maintained privacy between the front and back. With the high wall of the house close to the boundary fence, a pergola was designed to scale down the height over the path and a water feature was installed for interest and to create a focal point.

DRIVEWAY and FRONT GARDEN

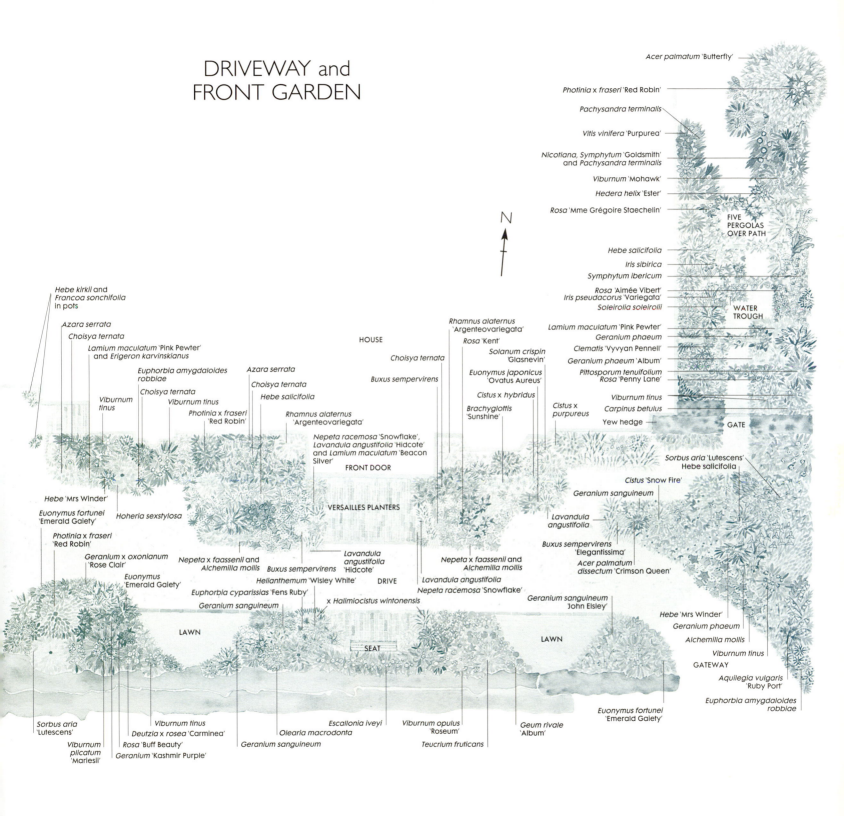

Acer palmatum 'Butterfly'

Photinia x fraseri 'Red Robin'

Pachysandra terminalis

Vitis vinifera 'Purpurea'

Nicotiana, Symphytum 'Goldsmith' and Pachysandra terminalis

Viburnum 'Mohawk'

Hedera helix 'Ester'

Rosa 'Mme Grégoire Staechelin'

FIVE PERGOLAS OVER PATH

Hebe salicifolia

Iris sibirica

Symphytum ibericum

Rosa 'Aimée Vibert'
Iris pseudacorus 'Variegata'

Soleirolia soleirolii

WATER TROUGH

Lamium maculatum 'Pink Pewter'

Geranium phaeum

Clematis 'Vyvyan Pennell'

Geranium phaeum 'Album'

Pittosporum tenuifolium
Rosa 'Penny Lane'

Viburnum tinus

Carpinus betulus

Yew hedge

GATE

N

HOUSE

Hebe kirkii and
Francoa sonchifolia
in pots

Azara serrata

Choisya ternata

Lamium maculatum 'Pink Pewter'
and Erigeron karvinskianus

Euphorbia amygdaloides
robbiae

Choisya ternata

Viburnum
tinus

Viburnum tinus

Photinia x fraseri
'Red Robin'

Azara serrata

Choisya ternata

Hebe salicifolia

Rhamnus alaternus
'Argenteovariegata'

Rhamnus alaternus
'Argenteovariegata'

Rosa 'Kent'

Choisya ternata

Solanum crispin
'Glasnevin'

Buxus sempervirens

Euonymus japonicus
'Ovatus Aureus'

Cistus x hybridus

Brachyglottis
'Sunshine'

Cistus x
purpureus

Sorbus aria 'Lutescens'
Hebe salicifolia

Cistus 'Snow Fire'

Nepeta racemosa 'Snowflake',
Lavandula angustifolia 'Hidcote'
and Lamium maculatum 'Beacon
Silver'

FRONT DOOR

Geranium sanguineum

VERSAILLES PLANTERS

Lavandula
angustifolia

Hebe 'Mrs Winder'

Euonymus fortunei
'Emerald Gaiety'

Hoheria sexstylosa

Buxus sempervirens
'Elegantissima'

Acer palmatum
dissectum 'Crimson Queen'

Photinia x fraseri
'Red Robin'

Geranium x oxonianum
'Rose Clair'

Euonymus
'Emerald Gaiety'

Nepeta x faassenii and
Alchemilla mollis

Lavandula
angustifolia
'Hidcote'

Buxus sempervirens

Nepeta x faassenii and
Alchemilla mollis

Helianthemum 'Wisley White'

DRIVE

Lavandula angustifolia

Euphorbia cyparissias 'Fens Ruby'

Nepeta racemosa 'Snowflake'

Geranium sanguineum

x Halimiocistus wintonensis

Geranium sanguineum
'John Elsley'

Hebe 'Mrs Winder'

Geranium phaeum

Alchemilla mollis

Viburnum tinus

GATEWAY

LAWN

SEAT

LAWN

Aquilegia vulgaris
'Ruby Port'

Sorbus aria
'Lutescens'

Viburnum
plicatum
'Mariesii'

Viburnum tinus

Deutzia x rosea 'Carminea'

Rosa 'Buff Beauty'

Geranium 'Kashmir Purple'

Geranium sanguineum

Olearia macrodonta

Escallonia iveyi

Viburnum opulus
'Roseum'

Teucrium fruticans

Geum rivale
'Album'

Euonymus fortunei
'Emerald Gaiety'

Euphorbia amygdaloides
robbiae

SPECIAL FEATURES

First impressions are always important and it is normally the front driveway of a house that creates the first impression for a visitor, so most homeowners want this to appear welcoming. The features in this front garden are quite plain and simple, avoiding fussiness and the use of too many different materials. The key area is around the front door where old bricks were laid to form a wide and inviting pathway with ample space for plants to flow over the edge and room for planters positioned either side of the front door. The planters contain bay, for year-round evergreen structure, with seasonal underplanting that is changed two or three times a year. The brick path is continued on the opposite side of the drive and provides space for a seating area using a simple hardwood bench surrounded with planting. On either side of the bench are terracotta pots that provide depth to the seating area when viewed from the front door. The seating area is primarily to be looked upon from the house rather than a space where one would sit and read a book. However, it is also quite useful to have a comfortable seat close to the front door.

Lavandula 'Hidcote' lines the brick path to the front door, underplanted with *Alchemilla mollis*, *Nepeta* x *faassenii* and *Nepeta* 'Snowflake'.

Gravel and brick

The largest feature of all is the drive itself, which is kept deliberately understated by avoiding the use of tarmac or block paving. Gravel is both practical and attractive. In this case we used 5mm (¼in) sharp grit that was rolled into tar sprayed on a base coat of tarmac. During hot weather the tar will tend to seep through in patches and a spare bag or two of grit is kept aside to sprinkle over these areas. Although the drive will last for many years with this minimal maintenance, it is necessary to renew the topping every four or five years to maintain a pristine appearance. Another advantage of a gravel drive is the security it gives in being able to hear arrivals on quite a noisy surface. There is a steep slope in one entrance of this 'in and out' driveway that required the use of tarmac spray to bond the gravel and prevent it from moving down the slope. Otherwise, on a level area, the gravel could have been rolled on to a base of hoggin material.

For continuity with the house the drive was edged with reclaimed bricks. These are engineering bricks hard enough to withstand hard frosts and tough enough to allow light cars and vans to run over the edge without damage. A heavier duty alternative would have been granite setts. However, this would have meant introducing yet another material and so losing continuity. By limiting the materials to bricks and gravel a unity is maintained. Where heavy use is likely outside the back door and garage the same brick was used as a paving material.

Shallow steps

Although the front door is the central feature, the side door close to the garage is in more regular use. Shallow steps were constructed in the same reclaimed brick, with an oak rail for safety and security providing a degree of enclosure for the entrance to the side door.

Geranium clarkei 'Kashmir Purple' and *Rosa* 'Buff Beauty' combine to give summer colour. *Viburnum* 'Lanarth' at the back has finished flowering and *Helianthemum* 'Wisley Primrose' provides a pale yellow cushion at the front.

Generous, wide steps allow space for clay pots to be placed at intervals leading down to the lower level and sweeping round to the drive to create a welcoming appearance and softening the house walls, steps and drive – the ideal spot for a little ornamentation.

Access from the front drive to the back garden is, as with many properties, a narrow space between the house and the neighbouring boundary. A narrow gap can appear very uninviting and it was necessary to plan a layout to provide a pleasant approach with some interest along the way and a feeling of continuity from front to back.

Paths and pergolas

The front drive narrows to become a pathway, still using brick edges with a gravel surface, to a heavy wrought-iron gate. The edges of the path are stepped or offset, allowing for planting directly in front of the gate to provide subtle privacy without screening it completely. Through the gate the space narrows down to 3–4m (10–13ft), with the house wall on one side and a high fence on the other. Here the path is laid with reclaimed random rectangular York stone that is also used in the back garden. Five small pergolas attached to the house along the side wall help to create an intimate and enclosed atmosphere.

The oak timbers are 10x12cm (4x5in) section with curved tie pieces 12x5cm (5x2in). The cross timbers are attached to the house wall using a stainless steel 'T'-shaped bracket. It is important to use stainless steel or galvanized steel to avoid rust-coloured stain marks running down the wall. The 'T' bracket is bolted to the wall using heavy duty rawl bolts and the cross timber laid on the protruding part of the 'T'. The top timber has been recessed underneath to allow the bracket to sit flush with the underside of the top rail. A small block, approximately 20cm (8in) long, which is an exact copy of the pergola end detail in the shape of a lamb's tongue, is offered up to the underside of the 'T' bracket. The three elements are then bolted together using a long coach bolt down through the top rail, through the 'T' bracket and into a threaded nut fixed into the block underneath. Holes for the bolt are then capped off using small oak plugs. The small block underneath is purely for decoration and serves no structural function. It does, however, lend more solidity to the appearance of the junction of the pergola and house wall, appearing to be a bearer protruding from the wall on which the pergola beams sit.

It is worth bearing in mind that in some areas it may be necessary to obtain permission from the local authorities to fix a structure to your house, particularly if it is a listed building or in a conservation area.

Old pump

At the base of one of the wooden uprights of the pergola is a simple rustic water feature comprising an old-fashioned cast iron hand pump mounted on a very rustic old piece of timber. Underneath the pump is a rusty cast-iron trough set partially into the ground. A small submersible water pump sits in the base of this trough and is connected to an electricity supply positioned on the wall of the house in a waterproof socket. Water is continually pumped through a pipe from the trough to the cast-iron hand pump and then flows back into the trough, providing the sound of running water and some movement in this part of the garden. To enhance the natural look of this feature and provide more movement, a small quantity of duckweed floats on the surface of the water.

Right Water is circulated through this old cast-iron pump into a trough partially buried in the bed. The fresh green leaves of ferns and ivy soften the edges of the trough and blend the water feature with the surrounding planting.

Left An elegant wrought-iron gate set into a yew hedge connects the front and back gardens. The open style of the gate links the two areas and does not impose on the planting either side.

PLANTS and PLANTING

A strong evergreen structure was essential here for a reliable year-round base, so the large proportion of evergreen shrubs such as box, *Photinia* x *fraseri* 'Red Robin' and *Viburnum tinus* was greater perhaps than in other planting schemes. In addition, there was a number of established plants close to the house that provided a good backdrop. It was necessary to weave new planting around the existing to blend quickly and create a unified scheme. Existing plants included *Choisya ternata*, *Brachyglottis* 'Sunshine', *Rhamnus alaternus* 'Argenteovariegata' and *Euonymus japonicus* 'Ovatus Aureus'.

Planting is balanced either side of the front door with a line of *Lavandula* 'Hidcote' on each side of the path surrounded by *Alchemilla mollis* and *Nepeta racemosa* 'Snowflake'. As a background to the *Lavandula* 'Hidcote', *Euphorbia wulfenii* provides strong form all year with lime-green bracts in late spring and early summer fitting in well with the blue, green and white planting theme in this area.

Most of the planting in the drive area is in full sun all day and the soil is very well drained and stony. However, to the side of the house there is a lot of shade, especially at the base of a fence where it is also very dry. Here, drifts of *Euphorbia amygdaloides robbiae*, groundcover ivies such as *Hedera helix* 'Ester' and *H. h.* 'Tres Coupe', pulmonaria and symphytum were selected.

x *Halimiocistus wintonensis* cascades either side of the bench, which forms a focal point opposite the front door and draws attention from the drive. Below, the small creamy white flowers with yellow centres of *Helianthemum* 'Wisley White' flow on to the brick paving and around the empty clay pots. In the background, the dark evergreen leaves of *Escallonia iveyi* form a solid backdrop for the bench.

x *Halimiocistus wintonensis* (zone 8) is a relative of the cistus or sun rose. It is a bi-generic hybrid, a cross between a cistus and a halimium, hence the x before the name. The flowers are paper thin, saucer shaped and white, with a maroon circle around a yellow centre with greyish green soft-textured leaves. It will quickly grow to 60cm (2ft) high and 80cm (2½ft) wide in well-drained ground and full sun. Once established, it will withstand considerable drought. It is similar in many ways to helianthemum, which also requires good drainage and lots of sun.

Helianthemum 'Wisley Primrose' (zones 5–7), also known as the rock rose, is evergreen like the halimiocistus, though with a much smaller habit of about 30x45cm (12x18in). These flowers are creamy white with a yellow centre. All helianthemums are useful as edging plants and are good for hiding the leggy stems of taller plants behind. They are also popular as rock garden plants where they should be planted in groups, rather than simply dotted about, and pruned in early spring by one-third to remove old woody growth.

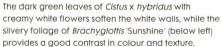

The dark green leaves of *Cistus* x *hybridus* with creamy white flowers soften the white walls, while the silvery foliage of *Brachyglottis* 'Sunshine' (below left) provides a good contrast in colour and texture.

Versailles planters with loosely clipped bay trees, *Laurus nobilis,* and a seasonal underplanting of white petunias. Blue globes of *Agapanthus* 'Headbourne Hybrids' stand out above the rest of the planting.

The soft yellow flowers of *Rosa* 'Buff Beauty' contrast with richly coloured *Geranium clarkei* 'Kashmir Purple'. *Helianthemum* 'Wisley Primrose' adds a pool of light yellow at the base of the rose.

Cistus x *hybridus (Cistus corbariensis)* (zones 7–9) is one of the hardiest cistus and is useful as evergreen structure as well as for its tissue paper thin white flowers with yellow centres. It grows to 90–120cm (3–4ft) high and up to 2m (6½ft) wide. The leaves are dark green and have a pinkish tinge during cold periods. The flower buds are also tinged pink. For best results, grow in well-drained, light soil in full sun. Pruning should be light and after flowering. On older plants, thin rather than trim to retain shape in spring. It is prone to bark split on wet soils during prolonged cold periods, so provide winter protection in frost pockets.

Laurus nobilis (zones 8–10), better know as the sweet bay or bay laurel, is an evergreen shrub that will grow to over 10m (35ft) if in the open ground and not pruned. It is more often used as a container plant trained into standards or cones for decoration or as a culinary herb. In containers it should be fed regularly during the growing season and clipped to encourage new growth. In milder climates it is a good evergreen screening shrub, even used as a hedge or windbreak. It responds well to pruning or trimming, either to shape or simply to restrict the size. The flowers are small yellowish white in late spring and it has black berries in autumn. The leaves are prone to wind scorch and in cold areas container-grown plants should be moved to a frost-free area.

Rosa 'Buff Beauty' (zones 5–10) is a hybrid musk rose, highly scented and very reliable. If planted by a post or fence it can grow to 3m (10ft). However, I prefer to use it as a free-standing shrub, supporting other plants under and around it such as *Nepeta racemosa* 'Walker's Low' and *Geranium clarkei* 'Kashmir Purple'. Grown as a shrub it can be pruned to 1.5x1.5m (5x5ft) and has attractive arching branches with young plum-coloured new shoots. Flowers appear in clusters regularly throughout the summer months, apricot at first fading to light buff yellow. Dark blue flowered perennials such as *Salvia* x *superba* and *Salvia* x *sylvestris* 'Mainacht' are excellent in combination with the new foliage and flowers of *Rosa* 'Buff Beauty'.

Powdery blue flowers of *Perovskia* 'Blue Spire' are surrounded by *Euphorbia wulfenii* in the foreground and in the background *Buxus sempervirens* (left) and *Lavandula angustifolia* 'Hidcote' (right).

The dark purple canopy of *Acer palmatum dissectum* 'Crimson Queen' rises above creamy white *Cistus* 'Snow Fire' to create a stunning combination.

A variegated ivy, *Hedera helix* 'Marginata Elegantissima', climbs up a pergola post in a shady part of the side garden and the dark green leaves of *Viburnum* 'Mohawk' provide a good backdrop.

Perovskia 'Blue Spire' (zones 5–9), known as Russian sage, is a useful late summer flowering sub shrub with white and grey stems, silvery, pungent leaves and plumes of violet-blue flowers. It will grow to 120x60cm (4x2ft) with a rather leggy habit and is best grown with other plants to act as support or in drifts of many plants in larger areas, otherwise it will require staking. Good companion plants are *Helenium* 'Moerheim Beauty', *Rosa* 'Buff Beauty', *Rosa* 'Graham Thomas' and *Geranium* 'Anne Thomson'. Grow in full sun and well-drained soil for best results. It will tolerate dry chalky conditions and even salt, so it is ideal for coastal gardens. The flowers, which appear in late summer, are best on new growth so older woody growth should be cut back very hard in spring.

Acer palmatum dissectum 'Crimson Queen' (zones 5–8) is one of many hundreds of varieties of Japanese maple, of which the palmate-leafed, dissected forms, with their light, feathery foliage, are very popular. 'Crimson Queen' is a good selection with finely cut foliage, crimson at first, turning rich purple during summer and crimson again in autumn. Ultimately reaching 2–2.4m (6–8ft) high and as wide, it is slow growing and requires moist, well-drained soil in sheltered dappled shade. The leaf colour is better in full sun but they may scorch during the hottest period of summer. The growth habit can be either a low mound or dome of foliage or, if trained up a stake into a tree shape, the top is a cascade of purple branches and can be more easily underplanted with groundcover.

Hedera helix 'Marginata Elegantissima' (zones 5–9) is a creamy white and green variegated form of ivy. The white variegation is tinged pink during winter. It grows in much the same way as common ivy though, as with all variegated plants, growth is slower than the green form due to the reduced amount of chlorophyll in the leaves. However, it can still be quite invasive and care is required to ensure that it does not cling to painted wood surfaces such as window frames. Its two main uses are as an evergreen and as a shade-tolerant climber. Plant on a shady fence or wall to give colour all year round and use it to lighten a dark corner. It is good to use with dark green shade-tolerant shrubs and groundcover such as *Choisya ternata*, *Skimmia japonica*, ferns and *Pachysandra terminalis*.

Here, purple-leafed *Berberis* x *ottawensis* 'Decora' in the background contrasts with the white walls. *Brachyglottis* 'Sunshine' is flanked with lime-green *Euphorbia wulfenii* (left) and *Alchemilla mollis* (right).

Francoa sonchifolia in pots line the steps to the side entrance with *Hebe* 'Kirkii' in the foreground. *Francoa sonchifolia* produces beautiful tall, slim spikes of flowers in midsummer (inset).

Berberis **x** *ottawensis* **'Decora'** (zones 4–8) is a large, arching, deciduous shrub with deep red/purple leaves and large thorns. Flowers are yellow and appear in late spring just as the leaves have formed. In autumn the branches are covered with red berries. Ultimate height and spread is 2.4x2.4m (8x8ft), though it can easily be kept smaller by hard pruning in spring. All berberis have thorns, some larger than others, and this is a variety recommended to deter vandals. Berberis all thrive best in full sun and, provided the soil is well drained, will tolerate most conditions including extreme cold and wind.

Francoa sonchifolia (zones 7–9) is a surprisingly underused plant. The long, evergreen/semi-evergreen leaves form a rosette never more than 30cm (1ft) high and from these rise spikes of flowers up to 1m (3ft) tall. Even in bud the flower spikes are attractive and the many small flowers on each spike are white but tinged pink with red markings. They flower during midsummer and require moist well-drained conditions in sun or part shade. I use them regularly in containers where they will look particularly good in terracotta pots placed in groups or for making a

'statement' either side of a door, gate or some steps. Because they are susceptible to extreme cold and may fail over winter, using them in containers has the advantage that they can be moved into a protected area during extreme cold. They can also be propagated easily by division in late spring or seed can be taken from the dead flower spikes in late summer. If sown in spring they will readily germinate to ensure that you have plants for next year, even if the original one is lost over winter.

TERRACED GARDEN

Designed on several levels with wide-ranging views, this garden is visible from all rooms of the house. Two levels of the terrace are regularly used for sitting and dining outside. They are surrounded by planting and provide views of rolling, tree-covered hills and fields. Three areas of lawn are linked in the lower part with a boundary of hedges and shrubbery. Closer to the house and terrace the planting becomes smaller scale and the paving is edged by mounds of plants spreading and softening the join between changes in level.

PLANNING the GARDEN

For the owners, who had just moved in and were used to a very large garden, the house and the terrace of this property seemed very distant from the garden. The original terrace was on one level and had a drop in excess of 1m (3ft) down to the lawn. Sitting on the terrace it felt like the edge of a precipice and it was clear that the new terrace would require multiple levels to integrate it more satisfactorily with the garden below. The existing retaining walls over 60cm (2ft) in height seemed rather imposing, so in this case it was necessary to look at the alternatives to get from one level to the next without these and to replace the old terrace completely.

The lawn slopes up towards the house and this provides an easy alternative to the steps for access to the garden. This is important as the owners are retired and the garden has to cater for one with very limited mobility. It was necessary to provide a terrace with a comfortable seating area surrounded by planting, close to the house and with easy access to the rest of the garden.

As with most terraces connected to the house, the upper area is viewed for much of the year from indoors. The challenge was therefore to design a layout that provided sufficient space to sit out on while at the same time avoiding a view from the windows of a vast, boring expanse of concrete paving. This was achieved by breaking the terrace up into three areas: upper, intermediate, and steps that had a landing partway down and incorporated a wrought-iron handrail.

Bright pink flowers of *Lavatera* 'Bredon Springs', with a mature birch tree in the background surrounded by long meadow grass that has a mass of bulbs flowering in spring.

With fine views from the terrace, one wanted to choose planting that would not obscure them while providing a little shelter when seated outside. Unfortunately it was not possible to create beds against the house due to the drainage system, and for reasons of safety and maintenance I avoided using many planted containers on the terrace. However, by incorporating planted areas on each level it was possible to blur the edge of changes in level and bring the garden closer to the house.

The aspect is quite open to strong winds and is sunny all day. The soil is very light loam and stony, and is therefore very free draining and requires the addition of plenty of compost to improve moisture retention. There was a number of established shrubs and perennials in the lower beds that required pruning and had to be incorporated into the overall design. Radical changes had to be made to the layout, resulting in three main areas of lawn, one below the terrace and one either side, created by narrowing the width of the lawn in appropriate positions and enhancing the planting to form pinch points which then emphasize the open areas.

To the north and west the lawns are fringed with planted borders using shrubs that remain below the hedge level, which is 2.4m (8ft) high at most, to avoid blocking views. The area of lawn to the east of the terrace was left to grow long, allowing wildflowers to naturalize, and with a mown path leading to a seating area.

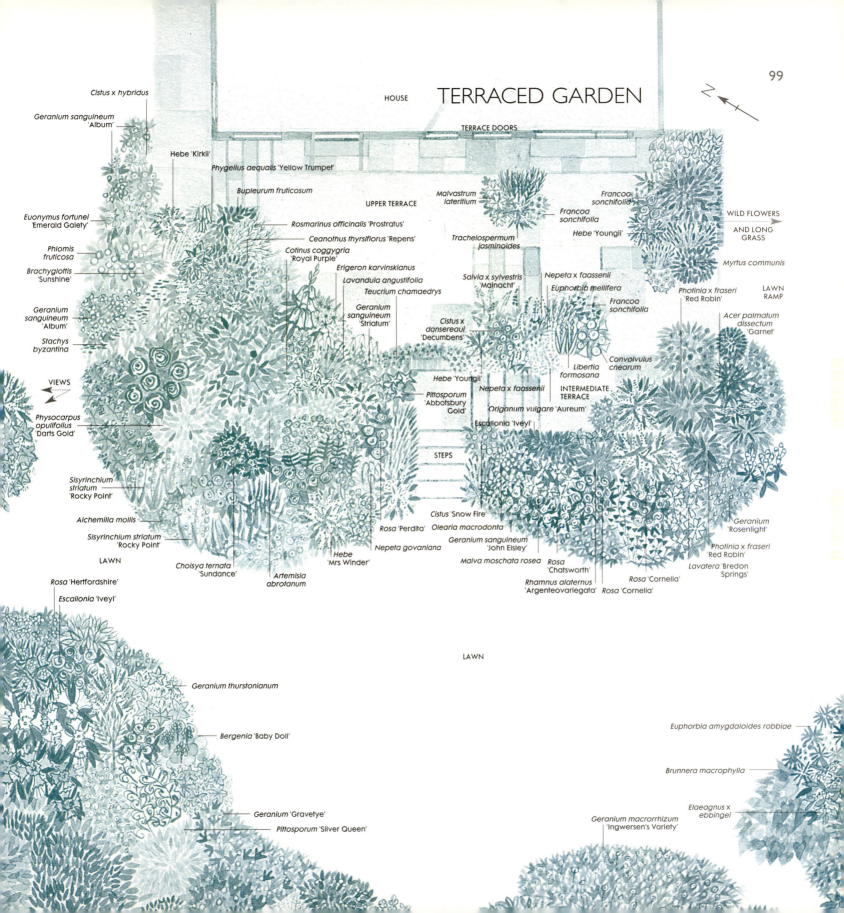

TERRACED GARDEN

HOUSE

Z

TERRACE DOORS

Cistus x hybridus

Geranium sanguineum 'Album'

Hebe 'Kirkii'

Phygelius aequalis 'Yellow Trumpet'

Bupleurum fruticosum

UPPER TERRACE

Malvastrum lateritium

Francoa sonchifolia

Francoa sonchifolia

Hebe 'Youngii'

WILD FLOWERS AND LONG GRASS

Euonymus fortunei 'Emerald Gaiety'

Rosmarinus officinalis 'Prostratus'

Ceanothus thyrsiflorus 'Repens'

Cotinus coggygria 'Royal Purple'

Trachelospermum jasminoides

Myrtus communis

Phlomis fruticosa

Erigeron karvinskianus

Salvia x sylvestris 'Mainacht'

Nepeta x faassenii

Euphorbia mellifera

Photinia x fraseri 'Red Robin'

LAWN RAMP

Brachyglottis 'Sunshine'

Lavandula angustifolia

Teucrium chamaedrys

Francoa sonchifolia

Acer palmatum dissectum 'Garnet'

Geranium sanguineum 'Album'

Geranium sanguineum 'Striatum'

Cistus x dansereaui 'Decumbens'

Stachys byzantina

Libertia formosana

Convolvulus cneorum

VIEWS

Hebe 'Youngii'

Nepeta x faassenii

INTERMEDIATE TERRACE

Physocarpus opulifolius 'Darts Gold'

Pittosporum 'Abbotsbury Gold'

Origanum vulgare 'Aureum'

Escallonia 'Iveyi'

STEPS

Sisyrinchium striatum 'Rocky Point'

Geranium 'Rosenlight'

Cistus 'Snow Fire'

Alchemilla mollis

Photinia x fraseri 'Red Robin'

Rosa 'Perdita'

Olearia macrodonta

Sisyrinchium striatum 'Rocky Point'

Nepeta govaniana

Geranium sanguineum 'John Elsley'

Rosa 'Chatsworth'

Lavatera 'Bredon Springs'

LAWN

Choisya ternata 'Sundance'

Hebe 'Mrs Winder'

Malva moschata rosea

Rosa 'Cornelia'

Rosa 'Hertfordshire'

Artemisia abrotanum

Rhamnus alaternus 'Argenteovariegata'

Rosa 'Cornelia'

Escallonia 'Iveyi'

Geranium thurstonianum

Euphorbia amygdaloides robbiae

LAWN

Bergenia 'Baby Doll'

Brunnera macrophylla

Geranium 'Gravetye'

Elaeagnus x ebbingei

Pittosporum 'Silver Queen'

Geranium macrorrhizum 'Ingwersen's Variety'

SPECIAL FEATURES

One of the most difficult challenges to overcome when planning and constructing any garden is how to deal with changes in level. It is also difficult to express this on a plan and it often tests the imagination and drawing skills during the process. The key features to draw attention to in this garden are the various methods of dealing with the changes in level from the patio doors, out on to the terrace and down to the lawn at the lower level. The problem with terracing a slope is that when viewed from the house, the terrace often feels like the edge of the world and the whole upper level appears to fall away to nothing. In addition, when looking back towards the house it can look perched and unconnected with the garden. To overcome this problem here, the majority of the steps move across the slope rather than directly down it. This also creates space for planting on each level, integrating the garden with the paved terrace and steps.

A gentle flight of steps leads up from the lawn to the terrace. Halfway up, a small landing marks the change in direction to the intermediate level of terrace.

Below The terrace is paved with a light grey concrete paving material, using five different sizes of rectangular slabs with a textured finish and planting to soften the edges.

Right The upper terrace is in an elevated position to enjoy the views, with plenty of room for a dining table and chairs and is surrounded by planting.

Paving

It was decided to use good quality concrete paving of a charcoal grey colour. With up to five different sizes used, the surface was more interesting than simply using uniform squares or rectangles. Most paving is now available in a mix of different-sized squares and rectangles and it is best to avoid cutting wherever possible. Edges to the terrace are constructed in brick, as are the risers to the steps, to tie in with the brick of the house.

There are two separate areas of paving linked by a shallow step: the larger upper terrace for a dining table and chairs and the intermediate terrace, which can be used for a small table and a couple of chairs to sit out to have coffee. The paved areas needed to have distinct differences between the space to dwell and the space to pass through. The latter should be narrow enough to exaggerate the former, otherwise the lack of distinction makes the space look very boring. So this terrace has been divided into an upper larger level, wide shallow steps, an intermediate smaller level and two pathways. The lawn is ramped up to the intermediate level to allow easy access, avoiding a flight of steps, ideal for wheelbarrows and wheelchairs and to access the upper part of the garden. The main flight of steps from the smaller lower level to the lower lawn has a wrought-iron handrail and, by positioning this on the lower set of steps,

Left *Escallonia* 'Iveyi' pushes through the wrought-iron handrail from the lower level. Tall stems of *Verbena bonariensis* topped with heads of purplish blue vie for space with pale pink *Malva moschata rosea*.

it is below eye level from the house and indeed mainly masked by the planting on the upper terrace. Richly planted beds containing combinations of *Euphorbia mellifera* surrounded by *Nepeta* × *faassenii* and *Salvia sylvestris* 'Mainacht' produce a rich mix of lime green, powder blue and purplish blue. The transition between levels is also enhanced by repetitive planting. For example, *Photinia* 'Red Robin' is positioned on the corner of the middle terrace and another one on the lower level. After a short while and with regular pruning they will grow in together as if creating one plant growing on the same level.

The wrought-iron handrail, made by a local blacksmith, extends beyond the top step to include part of the small intermediate terrace and slopes down to the paving, avoiding an abrupt end. It is painted traditional black gloss but could have been finished in a soft shade of grey, blue, green or red to complement the planting.

Above The dark purple foliage of *Cotinus coggygria* 'Royal Purple' is a good background for pale pink roses and *Geranium sanguineum* and provides some shelter when using the terrace for afternoon refreshments.

PLANTS and PLANTING

There were a number of established shrubs in the perimeter beds of this garden, including hydrangea, skimmia, hypericum, azalea, rhododendron, philadelphus and berberis. Many of these required a thorough pruning before they were integrated within the reshaped beds, and for a time the new planting was out of scale with the existing. This was partly overcome by using several specimen plants brought to the front of the newly shaped beds to cover the join between old and new planting. Also some of the existing shrubs were removed and groundcover drifted in from the front through to the middle of the beds, which added to the established look and helped to tie all the planting in together.

Around the terrace there was only one shrub I wanted to retain, *Cotinus coggygria* 'Royal Purple', which was pruned, fed and underplanted with shade-loving *Geranium nodosum*. This large shrub was, when viewed from the terrace, still low enough to avoid blocking the views to the west and, for contrast, silvers and yellows of *Stachys byzantina*, *Phlomis fruticosa* and *Physocarpus* 'Darts Gold' were planted in the same bed to link up with the similar shrubs and perennials on the opposite side of the lawn, providing continuity between the terrace and garden. On the eastern side where the lawn ramps up to the house, the grass was allowed to grow and pathways mown through to give an orchard feel where, in the spring, there are drifts of daffodils. This reduces maintenance and makes the garden more interesting.

Ceanothus 'Joyce Coulter' and *Rosmarinus officinalis* 'Prostratus' flow over the edges of the upper terrace.

Trachelospermum jasminoides covers the brick pillar with shiny evergreen leaves and scented white flowers.

Ceanothus 'Joyce Coulter' (zones 8–10), also known as the Californian lilac, has a wide spreading habit and evergreen leaves. It has an ultimate height of between 50cm (18in) and 1m (3ft) and a spread of up to 2m (6½ft). Prune all ceanothus immediately after flowering to encourage new growth that will flower the following year. The light blue flowers start in late spring and continue until early summer. It is tolerant of wind and will withstand a degree or so of frost, possibly more if in well-drained soil. It is particularly tolerant of drought conditions once established and combines well with *Rosmarinus officinalis* 'Prostratus' (zones 7–10). This variety has leaves that equal the common rosemary for flavour and scent. As its name suggests, the habit is low and spreading, making it a useful plant to soften the edges of paving. It requires full sun and good drainage to thrive.

Trachelospermum jasminoides (zones 8–10) is a most useful plant because it is a scented white-flowered evergreen climber. It will grow slowly up to 6m (20ft), though is easily pruned and can be kept to 3m (10ft). It requires full sun and well-drained soils though I have had success growing it on shady walls – just expect fewer flowers if grown out of the sun. The creamy white starry flowers have a jasmine scent, early to midsummer, and the dark green leaves often turn red during autumn and winter. Red foliage at other times is an indication that the plant requires food and water. To train on a wall or fence, trachelospermum is best tied to wires where its shoots will twine and eventually support itself (see page 139).

Planting flows from one level to the next. Top right is *Euphorbia mellifera* with the grassy leaves of *Libertia formosa* below and the silvery grey foliage of *Convolvulus cneorum* spilling out over the paving.

Alongside the steps dark mauve spikes of *Salvia* x *sylvestris* 'Mainacht' are accentuated by the delicate white flowers of *Cistus* x *dansereaui* 'Decumbens' behind and the pale violet flowers of *Hebe* 'Youngii'.

A golden corner with *Lavandula angustifolia* 'Rosea' in the foreground and the soft yellow flowers of *Rosa* 'Amber Queen' linking the stronger yellows of *Brachyglottis* 'Sunshine'.

Euphorbia mellifera (zones 8–10) is a shrubby variety of what is known as spurge and related to the poinsettia. It requires a sunny, well-drained position and will only tolerate a few degrees of frost. If allowed to grow unchecked, it will reach a rather straggly 2x2m (6½x6½ft). The main attribute of this euphorbia is its fresh green leaves with a light veining down the centre of the leaf. During early summer these are topped with sticky honey-coloured flowers that form pods later in summer. During hot weather these pods can be heard popping in the heat, catapulting hard black seeds that germinate readily. It is best pruned every few years by removing the old stems completely and bringing the canopy level down to new shoots springing from the base, in the same way that *Euphorbia wulfenii* is cut every year (see page 137).

Salvia x *sylvestris* 'Mainacht' (zones 4–8) is a very popular garden plant due to its intense dark violet-blue colour. It requires very good drainage to survive over winter and is otherwise quite hardy. As a herbaceous perennial salvia disappears completely during winter, forming a rosette of leaves in late spring or early summer followed by flowers during the summer. Its flower spikes rise 60cm (2ft) high and it forms a clump of similar width. Even the dead heads are attractive although as they turn brown it is best to cut them down to the base and encourage a second flush of flower for late summer. *Hebe* 'Youngii' (zones 8–9) likes full sun and is a very hardy variety that makes an evergreen mound of 30x45cm (12x18in) with pale violet flowers in early summer.

Lavandula angustifolia 'Rosea' (zones 5–9) is a pale pink form of lavender reaching about 60cm (2ft) high with a compact habit. As with all lavenders it requires good drainage and full sun and benefits from a gentle trim twice a year, first early in spring and again when the flowers are over. *Brachyglottis* 'Sunshine' (zones 8–10) is a silver-leafed shrub, attaining 1m (3ft) in height and 1.5m (5ft) in width. Thriving in most well-drained soils, it requires full sun, little maintenance and the bright yellow daisy flowers provide a splash of colour during midsummer. A year or so after planting brachyglottis can become rather straggly and will require hard pruning in spring. Regular trimming in late summer ensures it retains a good compact habit.

The soft yellow flowers of *Phlomis fruticosa* will light up any border throughout the summer.

Teucrium chamaedrys smothered in rose-pink flowers, with the white daisy flowers of *Erigeron karvinskianus* on the edge of the paving.

The tall vigorous stems of *Bupleureum fruticosum* topped with lime-green flowers and *Phygelius aequalis* 'Yellow Trumpet' in the foreground.

Phlomis fruticosa (zones 8–10), also known as Jerusalem sage, is an evergreen Mediterranean shrub with large, elliptical, hairy, grey-green leaves. It grows quickly to a height and spread of 1.2m (4ft) and soft yellow, hooded flowers continue from early to midsummer. To avoid woody, leggy stems, prune flowered branches close to the base in spring. The soil should be well drained and the aspect sunny and sheltered.

Teucrium chamaedrys (zones 5–9), also known as wall germander, is a dwarf bushy shrub reaching 30cm (1ft) high and 60cm (2ft) across. Thriving in a well-drained sunny position it is ideal on this raised terrace where bees are attracted in profusion by its rose-pink flowers during mid- to late summer. The foliage is aromatic and, as its name suggests, this plant is ideal to grow in or on top of walls. It is perfect for a narrow run of planting where the combination of different varieties would look patchy. It can also be used to form a low evergreen hedge in sheltered areas and, with a creeping rootstock habit, can be trimmed hard every year in late spring. Propagation is easy with softwood cuttings in early summer.

Bupleureum fruticosum (zones 6–7) is normally raised from seed and is not widely grown or readily obtainable. This umbelliferous plant (a member of the cow parsley family) will grow in the open but grows best against a sheltered wall or fence where it can reach a height of 2–2.5m (6½–8½ft). Its vigorous upright stems have glaucous blue leaves with a distinct white vein and by midsummer large heads of lime-green flowers make it a very architectural plant. It responds well to cutting back hard, which is fortunate as it can become rather woody and bare at the base if not pruned regularly. It is said to be easily raised from cuttings but I have had limited success. The cuttings need to be just in the right condition, not too soft and not too woody, so mid- to late summer should be the best time for propagation.

The dark leaves of *Cotinus coggygria* 'Royal Purple' with the double-flowered *Clematis viticella* 'Purpurea Plena Elegans' tumbling through its branches.

Malva moschata rosea erupts through the evergreen holly-like leaves of *Olearia* x *macrodonta*. Bright pink *Rosa* 'Chatsworth' are in the foreground.

The lush green, upright growth of *Artemisia abrotanum* is a good contrast to the lime-green leaves of *Choisya ternata* 'Sundance'.

Cotinus coggygria 'Royal Purple' (zones 5–8), also known as the smoke bush, is a deciduous shrub with round dark purple leaves that are great for dramatic contrasts. The plumy flowers are rather insignificant and normally only produced on older branches. Cotinus thrives on most soils and is very hardy, growing to 3–4m (10–12ft). With regular pruning it can be kept at around 2–2.5m (6½–8½ft). *Clematis viticella* 'Purpurea Plena Elegans' (zones 3–11) has striking small double-violet flowers in large clusters. I often use it to scramble through shrubs as it does here with the purple cotinus. This clematis is in group 3, which means that flowering is during mid- to late summer and therefore pruning should be carried out late winter or early spring.

Malva moschata rosea (zones 3–8) is a short-lived perennial that grows to 2m (3ft) high and has masses of saucer-shaped pale pink flowers from early summer through to autumn. As the flowers fade on each stem it can be removed to the base, which will encourage new growth. It can be quite invasive in a half-hearted sort of way. The aspect needs to be sunny and warm and it may need staking unless supported by surrounding plants such as shrub roses. Given fertile well-drained soil the clump will quickly spread and there is a danger of smothering longer term plants, so do not be afraid of pulling out a few stems to keep it under control. However, it is an excellent plant to provide a splash of soft pink summer colour over a long period.

Artemisia abrotanum (zones 4–9) has light green feathery foliage and is very aromatic when touched. The flowers are rather insignificant but the plant is worth growing for its foliage alone as the lush green colour is a good foil for many plant combinations. It requires full sun and good drainage and must be cut back hard every spring to promote a vigorous bushy habit, growing to 1m (3ft) high and up to 1m (3ft) wide. *Choisya ternata* 'Sundance' (zones 8–10) is a relatively new introduction. In full sun it has bright golden foliage though is better grown in light shade to prevent leaf scorch. Out of the sun the leaves become lime green, which I prefer, and it is a useful evergreen shrub growing to approximately 1.5m (5ft). It requires fertile well-drained soil and is also content to be grown as a container plant.

COURTYARD GARDEN

As a self-contained area, this courtyard is formed by the house and conservatory on one side and garden walls and a gravel drive on the other. The gravel drive is edged with box plants and pleached hornbeam to provide privacy, while the planting within the courtyard is restricted to a narrow selection of varieties, which increases impact and creates a restful atmosphere enhanced by the water feature. The conservatory dominates and is contemporary in style but built with traditional materials. The garden reflects this old and new and has a simplicity that rests easily with the surroundings.

PLANNING the GARDEN

Enclosed on two sides by a conservatory, on the third by a driveway and on the fourth by a wall, this courtyard is roughly square. It has to fulfil several requirements but be kept simple and unfussy. It is viewed all year round from the conservatory and windows above. It is also a busy thoroughfare for access to the main garden. Apart from the house itself the surrounding structures are new and the area was completely clear of any planting.

The style of conservatory meant that the roof gutter was not adequate to take much rain water and therefore an open gully with a metal grille, approximately 30cm (1ft) wide, ran the full length of the exterior conservatory wall to carry the water away. This had to be incorporated within the garden layout and attention drawn away from it, or at least it needed to be softened by planting.

With the courtyard enclosed on three sides it was possible that water would collect in this area and cause waterlogging problems for the planting. Therefore, a system of drainage had to be devised. This was particularly important as the property has a high water table due to a nearby river. It was decided to dig a sump, which would take the form of a manhole, and if the water level rose to excess during winter, a submersible pump could be used to reduce the level. The soil is stony and alkaline with clay below, and no amount of digging out and replacement of soil would help ease a possible drainage problem. When viewed from the conservatory the courtyard planting had to remain low level. Some form of enclosure on the open side was required, not only because of the

Focal points within the courtyard invite you through the heavy oak doorway.

driveway, but also a neighbouring property that overlooked this area. The wall opposite the conservatory, whilst very attractive Cotswold stone, also needed some form of light screening to provide depth, using height in the foreground. This was not a suitable area for using small numbers of a wide range of materials and plants – it is far better to use groups of the same type. It also helped to minimize maintenance, which was an important consideration.

Access was always going to be necessary through planted areas and a series of 'stepping stone' paving slabs was laid in the bed between the tank and conservatory. However, it was important that these 'disappear' and not impact on the planting layout or give the appearance of a path. They were therefore randomly placed after the planting was done.

Between the conservatory and the gravel drive it was necessary to create space to park a small car to unload shopping. At other times this space should look attractive and unlike a car-parking space. Close to this area was an old brick pottery kiln that, since this is a listed building, could not be altered in any way. It was important to incorporate this at least into the planting scheme within the confines of the existing shape.

The aspect of this garden is quite sunny and sheltered from wind, though prone to heavy frosts in the winter. As a sheltered area, the courtyard was ideal for sitting out in good weather with a cup of tea and the Sunday newspapers so space for a table and some chairs also had to be included in the plan.

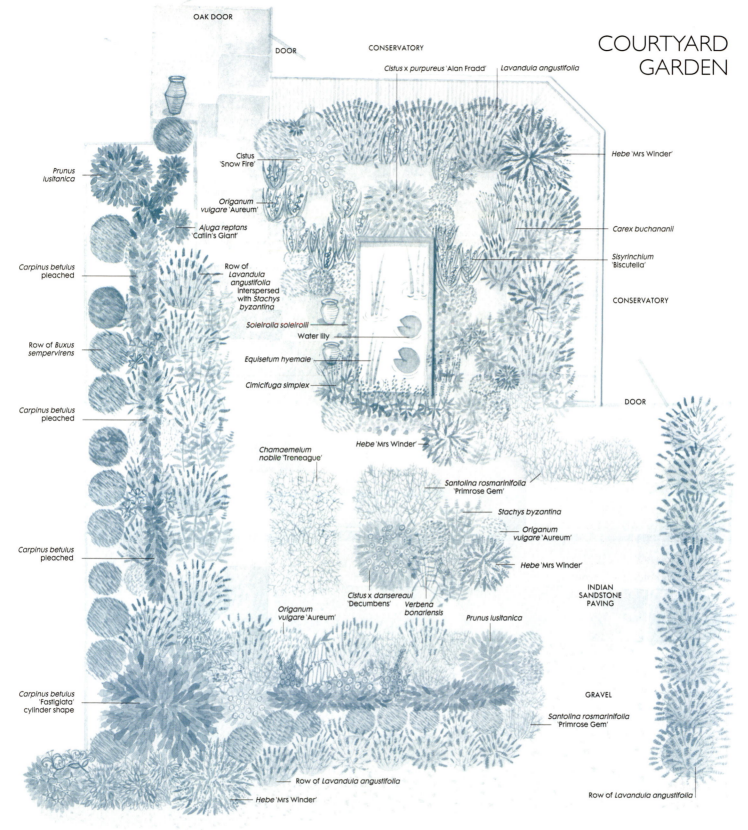

OAK DOOR

DOOR

CONSERVATORY

Cistus x purpureus 'Alan Fradd'

Lavandula angustifolia

Hebe 'Mrs Winder'

Prunus lusitanica

Cistus 'Snow Fire'

Origanum vulgare 'Aureum'

Ajuga reptans 'Catlin's Giant'

Carpinus betulus pleached

Row of Lavandula angustifolia interspersed with Stachys byzantina

Carex buchananii

Sisyrinchium 'Biscutella'

CONSERVATORY

Row of Buxus sempervirens

Soleirolia soleirolii

Water lily

Equisetum hyemale

Carpinus betulus pleached

Cimicifuga simplex

DOOR

Hebe 'Mrs Winder'

Chamaemelum nobile 'Treneague'

Santolina rosmarinifolia 'Primrose Gem'

Stachys byzantina

Origanum vulgare 'Aureum'

Carpinus betulus pleached

Hebe 'Mrs Winder'

INDIAN SANDSTONE PAVING

Origanum vulgare 'Aureum'

Cistus x dansereaui 'Decumbens'

Verbena bonariensis

Prunus lusitanica

Carpinus betulus 'Fastigiata' cylinder shape

GRAVEL

Santolina rosmarinifolia 'Primrose Gem'

Row of Lavandula angustifolia

Hebe 'Mrs Winder'

Row of Lavandula angustifolia

SPECIAL FEATURES

With a heavy structure of walls and a conservatory surrounding this courtyard, what this garden really needed was a strong focal point. I created this with a water feature constructed from an old galvanized tank, which in its former days had been a cold water header tank for a large building.

Water tank feature

Originally obtained from a farm sale, this tank was first used in my exhibit at the Chelsea Flower Show in 2002 and afterwards seemed appropriate for this garden. Indeed during the Flower Show I received a text message from my client: 'How about the water feature for our new garden?' Fortunately it was perfectly suited and in the end the rest of this courtyard garden was designed around it. It is rare that a show garden can be relocated satisfactorily unless originally designed for a specific location, but individual features, like this one, from flower shows are often used with great success. The tank is 2.4m (8ft) long and 1.2m (4ft) wide with a depth of 45cm (18in) and is sited in the centre of the courtyard garden to unify the courtyard and conservatory.

With some modification it was converted into a restful water feature. The encrusted scale was scraped out from the inside and a thick black waterproof sealant painted inside on the bottom and sides. A new metal tank of similar dimensions but approximately 7.5cm (3in) wider all round was constructed and positioned in a hole in the ground, ensuring that it was

Right The central feature of this garden is a galvanized tank running with water and planted simply.

Left A shimmering sheet of water reflects the surrounding planting. *Equisetum hyemale* and a small variety of water lily planted in the tank do not interfere with the gentle water flow. Mind-your-own-business, newly planted around the tank, will soon surround and smother the stone edges with a pleasing green cushion of leaves.

level. Within this tank concrete bearers are placed to support the old tank resting above, again absolutely level. The base of the top tank is about 1cm (½in) below the top edge of the reservoir tank, to avoid splashing and loss of water. A line of Cotswold stone blocks the size of an average brick were then set on edge slightly above the top edge of the lower reservoir tank and cemented firmly in place. One end of the tank was drilled and a supply pipe fitted with a gland to prevent leakage. This supply pipe runs along the bottom of the tank and feeds water out with even distribution.

The water is circulated by a submersible pump in the reservoir and fed into the top tank via the pipe at one end with a non-return valve to prevent water from flowing back and emptying the top tank. As the top tank overflows, the water gently runs over the sides and down into the reservoir below. The whole effect provides a shimmering reflective surface of water with gentle movement as the water flows over the edges. It may be necessary to top up the reservoir from time to time or a cistern could be installed to top it up automatically. This was not installed here but, provided there is a water supply close by, a permanent feed can be connected to a cistern sunk in the ground at the same level as the reservoir tank. When the level drops the ball valve will allow the water to top itself up.

If algae builds up in the tank, it will be necessary to try clearing it with algicide. Otherwise the top tank will need emptying out from time to time and refilling with fresh water.

Indian sandstone paving

The courtyard is an important access area from the drive to the main garden and is paved with rectangular Indian sandstone paving slabs. These vary in size, which makes an interesting surface, and the colour blends well with the Cotswold stone. This Indian stone is available in a number of colours from brown through to shades of pink, buff and grey so it is worth obtaining some samples before ordering. It is cheaper than English sandstone or new or reclaimed York stone and less slippery when wet. Another advantage is that it is available in a uniform thickness.

The paving is laid out in a stepped shape to take the path from the drive to the attractive solid oak door that leads to the main garden, allowing the planting to soften the edges. On one side, paving is laid close to the side of the water feature. On the other side, a few individual slabs are placed on a bed of concrete acting as stepping stones through the planting. These were laid after the planting was completed to be sure they would not interfere with planting where it was wanted.

Above Water flows gently over the edge of the tank.

Left Stone chippings surface the drive and the adjacent beds are edged with Cotswold stone blocks.

A square bed of non-flowering chamomile within the paving forms a pleasant mound of aromatic foliage.

Driveway

The drive is laid with stone chippings and these also act as a mulch for the planting in the drive area instead of making specific beds, which would visually narrow the drive at an already narrow point between buildings.

Chamomile bed

Two beds are included within the paved area and one is planted with chamomile to soften the paving and yet allow space for a small table and chair. The non-flowering chamomile must be used or it will grow too tall to tread upon.

PLANTS and PLANTING

Surrounded by walls on three sides and with a drive on the fourth, it was necessary to introduce some large structural plants before any detailed planting could be considered. Trained hornbeam, *Carpinus betulus,* was the solution, using pleached trees to soften the eaves and box, *Buxus sempervirens,* in groups of three along the base of the trees to soften the wall line and provide some evergreen structure. The pleached hornbeam are still quite new and will join up to form a continuous screen. At about 2–3m (6–10ft) high, a cylindrical hornbeam that is a clipped form of *Carpinus betulus* 'Fastigiata' is used as an 'anchor point'. In addition to the box plants at the base of the hornbeam, several other buxus shapes are used in crucial points for winter structure and *Prunus lusitanica,* Portugal laurel, will have to be regularly pruned to maintain a good compact shape.

The courtyard is designed to look good all year so the detailed planting also includes a large proportion of plants that have foliage all year round, including lavenders, thymes, hebes and santolina. The key to success with the choice of plants here is the use of a limited number of different varieties which is why box, lavender and santolina make up at least 60 per cent of the whole scheme. Colours are all soft and gentle to combine with the light-coloured stone walls and sandstone paving. The soil is light and free draining and the aspect sheltered with sun on all areas for most of the day.

The lime-green tubular flowers of *Phygelius aequalis* 'Yellow Trumpet' are surrounded by the pretty silvers and blues of lavender.

Phygelius aequalis 'Yellow Trumpet' (zones 7–9) has tubular lime-green flowers borne on green fleshy stems that grow up to 1m (3ft) high and flower from early summer to early autumn. Removal of the flowered stems as they finish encourages new growth and more flowers from the base. They should be treated rather like a hardy fuchsia and cut back hard every spring, if indeed the tops have not already been frosted to ground level. The ideal soil is moist, fertile and in a sheltered position. Over two or three years the centre may die out as the shoots spread out from the original plant and therefore it is worth renewing the plant from time to time to retain a bushy habit. Propagation is easy by softwood cuttings in early summer.

Mounds of box in groups of three have been allowed to grow in together. *Verbena bonariensis* and *Delphinium* 'Black Knight' grow in the background with a line of *Lavandula angustifolia* in the foreground.

Verbena bonariensis (zones 4–9) is a late-flowering summer perennial with heads of light purple flowers on tall wiry stems up to 1.5m (5ft). You will find it in many of my gardens or at least those with good drainage and plenty of sun. It seeds freely so just one or two of these plants introduced could produce an abundance by the following year, so look out for the seedlings when weeding. One of the great attributes of this plant is that it grows tall and yet you can easily see through it. It therefore combines readily with many other types of plant, providing the border with a stately presence. Bees and butterflies love it, but do not try to use it as a cut flower as the small heads will droop immediately once cut and put indoors.

In the foreground *Santolina rosmarinifolia* 'Primrose Gem' echoes the soft buff colours of the stone. The steely blue *Lavandula angustifolia* in the background softens the edge of the metal drainage grille.

The cylinder-shaped hornbeam forms a corner piece to the tree planting and softens the roof line. Soft green foliage is carried down to the *Chamaemelum nobile* 'Treneague' lawn (below right).

Spiky brown grass, *Carex buchananii*, mingles with *Lavandula angustifolia* in the background, with *Erigeron karvinskianus* providing a mound of white daisies in front.

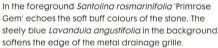

Santolina rosmarinifolia **'Primrose Gem'** (zones 7–10), commonly known as cotton lavender, is a dense sub-shrub growing to 60cm (2ft) with fresh green scented leaves. Flowers are produced on short spikes and are small, round and creamy yellow in colour during early to midsummer. It is a plant that may be used in a similar way to lavender, either as a small hedge or to soften corners and flow over the edge of paved areas. The colour of the flowers is soft enough to blend with the purples and blues of lavenders and hebes and the light greens of hornbeam, box and the sisyrinchium. They should be trimmed during late summer when the flowers finish, but unlike lavenders, should also be pruned hard in spring when they become straggly, to maintain a compact habit.

Chamaemelum nobile **'Treneague'** (zones 5–8) is better known as chamomile. This is the non-flowering form used for chamomile lawns. It can only be propagated by cuttings because as a non-flowering form it obviously does not produce seed. Soil conditions should be moist but well drained and in a sunny site. It is used here to provide a green surface within the paving where further planting would have taken too much space. It can be walked upon occasionally and releases a pleasant fragrance. Chamomile lawns can be difficult to keep in a good condition but in a small area they are easy to maintain and just require cutting back from time to time with a sharp pair of shears.

Carex buchananii (zones 7–9) with very narrow bronze leaves is a tough grass that grows to 60cm (2ft), and is very hardy and evergreen. The brown colouring works well with lavenders and reflects the light brown sandstone paving in this garden. In some situations it can simply look like a dead grass so care is needed when choosing its planting partners. *Erigeron karvinskianus* (zones 5–8) looks just like the common daisy when it first opens – white with a yellow centre. However, it quickly fades to light pink and then darker, producing a range of pink and white flowers all at the same time. It only grows 10–15cm (4–6in) high but will spread easily over edges of paving. This little plant will flower from early summer right through to late autumn and self-seed in cracks in paving where it can.

Hebe 'Mrs Winder' provides evergreen structure surrounded by *Stachys* 'Silver Carpet'.

Planting is kept low around the water feature. *Sisyrinchium striatum* grows in the background with a smaller version, *Sisyrinchium* 'Biscutella', to the left.

Carpinus betulus trained on a framework gives height to the surrounding greenery. Patches of lime-green *Origanum vulgare* 'Aureum' and *Phygelius aequalis* 'Yellow Trumpet' light up the planting.

Hebe **'Mrs Winder'** (zones 8–10) has attractive purplish leaves during winter, spring and early summer that gradually turn green during the growing season. During late summer violet-blue flowers in racemes cover this neat, dome-shaped plant that grows to 1m (3ft) high and 1.2m (4ft) wide. I use this plant regularly for good all-year-round structure and as an excellent foil for pinks, purples and silvers such as *Geranium sanguineum, Stachys byzantina* and *Nepeta* x *faassenii*. Unfortunately in recent years large-leafed hebes have suffered from mildew and this variety is no exception. While not the most susceptible, *Hebe* 'Mrs Winder' can suffer from this disease and the best solution is to cut off affected shoots and keep the plant well watered. The soil should be free draining and in full sun.

Sisyrinchium striatum (zones 7–10) has strap-like leaves with a spiky appearance and grey-green colour. They should be planted in groups of at least five or more with the odd one planted a short distance away from the main group, just as they would normally grow and seed in a natural situation. In mild areas they will remain evergreen; otherwise, by late winter the stems will have turned black and new shoots will appear from the base in the spring. The flowers appear during the early summer and are pale yellow above the spiky leaves, making the overall height 45–60cm (18–24in). The variety *Sisyrinchium* 'Biscutella' is much smaller, reaching only 15cm (6in), with slender grassy leaves and pretty, starry terracotta flowers. It echoes the brown *Carex buchananii* and shines out among the blues and purples.

Carpinus betulus **'Fastigiata'** (zones 4–7) is the European hornbeam and a member of the birch family, though slightly resembling a beech. It has twiggy growth and is easily trained or shaped either as a hedge or tree. Although deciduous the dense growth makes it effective screening even during winter and, left to grow naturally, it forms a dense symmetrical spreading tree. It requires moist but well-drained soil and in my experience I find it tolerates wet winter soils better than beech. In spring the leaves are an extremely fresh, light green colour, particularly attractive seen with the sun shining through them; in a good autumn they turn golden yellow. To form the cylinder on this tree the top has been trimmed flat and the sides rounded. The branches grow naturally in a radial fashion, lending itself to this form.

The spiky leaves of *Equisetum hyemale* provide a sharp contrast to the shimmering sheet of water flowing over the sides of the water tank.

Lavandula angustifolia grows in drifts along the back of the courtyard planting to soften the walls while remaining below the level of the windows.

A combination of *Thymus vulgaris* 'Silver Posie' (below right) with *Salvia officinalis* 'Purpurescens' and *Stachys byzantina* 'Silver Carpet' softening the edge of the paving.

Equisetum hyemale (zones 3–8) is known as the scouring rush and is used in this garden in the water tank, planted in shallow baskets with the root base just below the surface. It is useful as a simple, spiky form piercing the sheet of water of the tank and the reflections are striking on the smooth water surface. The roots should be covered by no more than 10cm (4in) of water. The evergreen stems are bright green and hollow with grey bands, at intervals, often with cones on the tips. In its natural habitat the rush, a relative of the horsetail or marestail, a pernicious weed in our gardens, will grow to at least 2m (6ft) high, so it is best grown in a controlled situation where it can be contained.

Lavandula angustifolia (zones 5–9) is the true English lavender with lavender-blue flowers and has given rise to many cultivars. The silver-grey foliage is useful for all-year-round interest and is very aromatic. By midsummer when the flower spikes are about to burst into colour the plant may have reached more than 60cm (2ft). It is one of the most hardy lavenders but still requires very free-draining soil to prevent rotting off during winter. Once established it is tolerant of drought. It is planted in drifts in this garden, which is the best way to use it, either as an informal, low hedge or in swathes for low-maintenance, high-impact groundcover. All lavender must be grown in full sun and the hotter the conditions the more highly scented the foliage becomes as the leaves produce oils to protect them from the sun.

Thymus vulgaris 'Silver Posie' (zones 7–9) is one of the most popular thymes, probably because of its habit and silvery white-edged leaves, which take on a pinkish tinge during winter. Small pink flowers appear from late spring to early summer and the foliage is very aromatic, as you would expect of a thyme. It should be trimmed hard in spring and lightly after flowering, otherwise the plant will become woody and the habit untidy. By midsummer it will have formed a cushion about 20x25cm (8x10in) and is a good edging plant used in combination with the silver-leafed *Artemisia* 'Powis Castle' or *Stachys byzantina* and the purple-leafed *Salvia officinalis* 'Purpurascens', which is the purple form of the herb sage, with matt, evergreen leaves and blue flowers in midsummer.

SECLUDED INTIMATE GARDEN

This small country garden has a cosy atmosphere and is crammed full of plants. The three access points and the path through the middle of the garden have not been allowed to dominate the space. The garden is designed to be used for three main purposes: as the approach to the house with front gate and path; as a place to relax and do nothing; and to contain a collection of interesting plants for the gardening enthusiast. The features include paving and pathways, water and lawn, and hedging and pergola, all combined and unified by a tapestry of planting.

PLANNING the GARDEN

This small garden, approximately 7x20m (23x65ft), receives a lot of sun and is on heavy clay soil. It is a relatively low-cost garden in that the hard construction was kept to a minimum and the features kept simple.

With four access points linked with a gravel path the primary purpose of the garden is to provide a cosy, comfortable area in which to sit and read, to escape from the outside world – and yet still to have a sense of space.

The main problems to overcome when designing this garden included very heavy soil conditions, so plenty of ground preparation was necessary. It is on a gentle slope that needs to be taken into account when building pathways.

To the east a rather ugly house gable end that tended to overpower the garden required masking without encroaching on the space available.

With a noisy road nearby and situated on a busy flight path, a water feature helps to divert attention from traffic and aircraft noise and this was achieved by using an old farm trough and a simple large brass tap with a circulating pump.

Designed for a very keen gardener, a wider range of unusual plants was used than is perhaps found in the average garden and the question of maintenance was not a problem. Although used mainly during the summer months, there is plenty of year-round structure provided by evergreen shrubs and groundcover, so there is some winter interest as well as continual colour from early summer until the autumn.

From an oak gate in the hornbeam hedge the gravel path leads through two pergola sections covered in roses to a small side gate made of wrought iron. The pergolas provide a sense of distance when sitting in the brick-paved area on the seat under the eaves of the house. The winding gravel path and sections of pergola create a pleasant vista even in this short length of garden. The pergolas also serve to provide privacy and enhance the soft curved shape of the path.

The boundary required solid screening and this is provided by a yew hedge to the west and hornbeam to the north. The hornbeam at the oak gate is planted double width and trained into an arch for additional screening and extra privacy. On the opposite side of the path from the water feature and brick paved area is a small area of lawn that can be used as a larger seating area for entertaining.

The view down the garden from the brick-paved area allows the eye to wander down the path and to take in the rose-clad pergola.

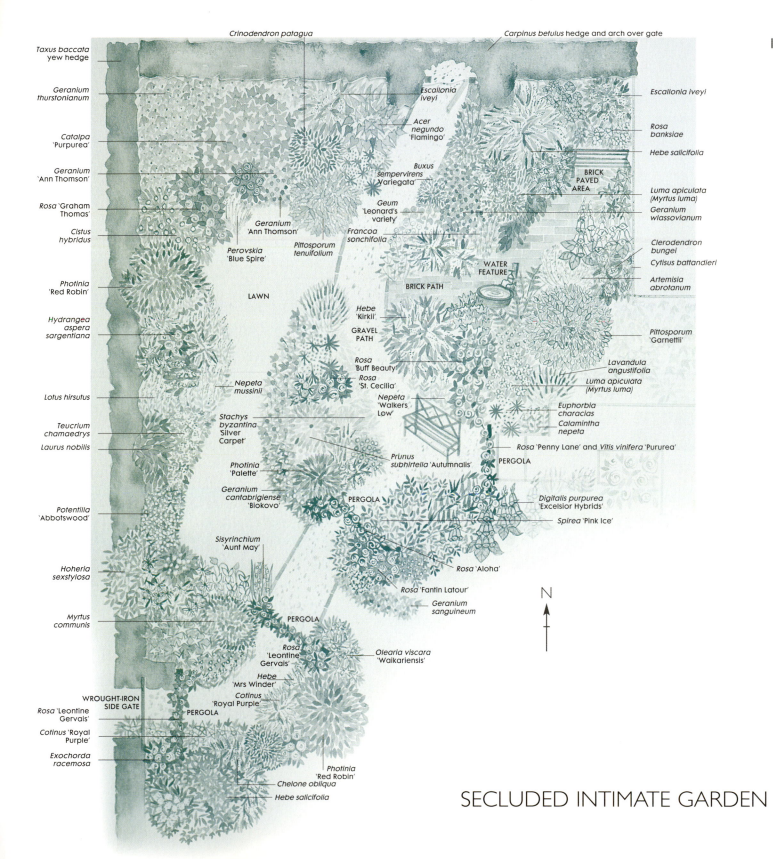

Crinodendron patagua

Carpinus betulus hedge and arch over gate

Taxus baccata yew hedge

Geranium thurstonianum

Catalpa 'Purpurea'

Geranium 'Ann Thomson'

Rosa 'Graham Thomas'

Cistus hybridus

Photinia 'Red Robin'

Hydrangea aspera sargentiana

Lotus hirsutus

Teucrium chamaedrys

Laurus nobilis

Potentilla 'Abbotswood'

Hoheria sexstylosa

Myrtus communis

WROUGHT-IRON SIDE GATE

Rosa 'Leontine Gervais'

Cotinus 'Royal Purple'

Exochorda racemosa

PERGOLA

Escallonia iveyi

Acer negundo 'Flamingo'

Buxus sempervirens 'Variegata'

Geum 'Leonard's variety'

Francoa sonchifolia

Geranium 'Ann Thomson'

Perovskia 'Blue Spire'

Pittosporum tenuifolium

LAWN

Hebe 'Kirkii'

GRAVEL PATH

Rosa 'Buff Beauty'

Rosa 'St. Cecilia'

Nepeta 'Walkers Low'

Nepeta mussinii

Stachys byzantina 'Silver Carpet'

Photinia 'Palette'

Geranium cantabrigiense 'Biokovo'

Prunus subhirtella 'Autumnalis'

PERGOLA

Sisyrinchium 'Aunt May'

PERGOLA

Rosa 'Leontine Gervais'

Hebe 'Mrs Winder'

Cotinus 'Royal Purple'

Olearia viscara 'Waikariensis'

Photinia 'Red Robin'

Chelone obliqua

Hebe salicifolia

Rosa 'Fantin Latour'

Rosa 'Aloha'

Geranium sanguineum

Escallonia iveyi

Rosa banksiae

Hebe salicifolia

BRICK PAVED AREA

Luma apiculata (Myrtus luma)

Geranium wlassovianum

Clerodendron bungei

Cytisus battandieri

Artemisia abrotanum

WATER FEATURE

BRICK PATH

Pittosporum 'Garnettii'

Lavandula angustifolia

Luma apiculata (Myrtus luma)

Euphorbia characias

Calamintha nepeta

Rosa 'Penny Lane' and Vitis vinifera 'Pururea'

PERGOLA

Digitalis purpurea 'Excelsior Hybrids'

Spirea 'Pink Ice'

N

SECLUDED INTIMATE GARDEN

SPECIAL FEATURES

The garden path is a dominant feature of this garden. Paths are one of the first elements to consider when planning the layout of any garden and they often establish the overall shape, linking the access points in and out of the garden. Paths should where possible follow closely the shortest route that would be taken if there were no planting. The position of trees and other features should be used to give purpose to changes in direction and the garden here is divided into useful spaces by the path. The ground slopes gently and a stone or concrete paved surface would not be appropriate. It could be slippery and would look like a ramp. A curved path using brick on a slope is acceptable and grass paths also work for a slope. However, for reasons of budget and practicability, I decided to create a gravel path, edged with brick. The brick edge contains the gravel and links with the brick of the house and informal brick-paved seating area.

Construction is simple. After first digging out the soil along the length of the path a brick edge is laid on a line of mortar that is then spread halfway up each brick on both sides to hold it firmly in place. The bricks are laid flat, end to end, and, for tight curves, they are cut in half to avoid wide joints between the bricks. When the cement is set firm a textile membrane is put in the bottom of the path and topped by a thick layer of scalpings or type 1 road-building base. This is a mixture of angular stone of varying sizes from 2cm (¾in) down to fine dust that, when compacted, provides a very firm base. This can either be compacted using a ramming tool or ideally a mechanical vibrating plate to ensure the base does not work up through the finished gravel surface. This base should be firmed to approximately 2cm (1in) below the top of the bricks to allow for a 1cm (⅜in) layer of shingle. In this case 1cm (⅜in) inland shingle was used as it was local to the area; derived from sandstone with an attractive brown colour, it is quite soft and easy to walk upon. The stones are fairly flat rather than the normal round shape of marine shingle and, therefore, pack down quite evenly and provide a firm surface. This makes an attractive, relatively cheap pathway that requires little maintenance except for topping up every year or so with some fresh shingle and weeding out the annual weed seedlings that establish themselves after a year or so. It has the advantage that garden plants also self-seed in the gravel and this has happened in several places where some aquilegias, foxgloves, geraniums, alchemilla, lychnis, salvia

Left A green oak pergola weathered to an attractive silver-grey colour, complements the rustic bench beneath.

Above A wrought-iron gate provides a welcome at the entrance to the garden. Foxgloves and aquilegias have self-seeded into the path, making the gate impossible to close, but fortunately it is more for decoration than security.

The gravel path is edged with bricks that have been cut in half to maintain a gentle curve. The foliage of *Stachys* 'Silver Carpet' softens the edge.

and euphorbia all have crept on to the pathway, blurring the join of the path and the garden and adding to the intended cosy atmosphere.

It is important that where the lawn joins the path edge the turf is just above the level of the brick for ease of mowing and safety. The lawn is about as small as can be practicable for easy mowing and maintenance but helps to give a sense of space within this small garden and provides an area for entertaining.

Brick paving

To give a firm base to the water feature and provide a surface for seating, a brick-paved area was also laid. This was constructed in a rather homemade fashion, partly for reasons of economy and urgency and also to be consistent with the required informal theme. A mixed collection of second-hand bricks was laid directly on the ground in an informal manner: that is,

A new oak table and chair on the brick-paved area provide a comfortable corner in which to sit and relax, surrounded by planting that cascades down the wall and over the pathway.

none of the edges was cut and no cement was used at any stage; they were simply tapped into place with a wooden block. The idea was to create a simple paved area that looked as if at some time it had been the floor of a building or yard, derelict, partly covered with soil and with plants flowing over the edges. This has resulted in many plants seeding themselves in the joints of the brickwork. Unfortunately weeds can also seed in the cracks and so regular maintenance is necessary. However, the result is still worth the effort. Indeed it is so informal that a few weeds do not even detract. The path has remained fairly even over a number of years and this is because the soil was thoroughly flattened and consolidated before the bricks were laid. It has the advantage that if at any time the shape is to be altered this can be done by simply adding a few more bricks or taking some up. It has proved quite adequate for light use though the bricks on the edge may rock when walked upon.

Water feature

With a flight path overhead and traffic noise in the background, a water feature with the sound of running water provides a welcome distraction. In keeping with the rustic theme, an old glazed feeding trough from a cowshed was used to contain the water. Set partially into the ground close to the brick-paved area, it must have originally been a corner trough, having two straight sides with a curve at the front. Because the garden is on a gentle slope and the ground was dug out to lay the brick paving on a fairly level and even surface, the trough acted as a 'retaining wall' in this part of the garden with the soil banked up on two sides. It was crucial to ensure that the base on which it sat was level and a solid base of concrete was poured in to ensure it did not sink. I wanted the water to give the effect of always brimming at the top. An old brass tap mounted on a rustic oak stake was connected to a piece of copper pipe that in turn has a plastic tube clipped to it. The plastic tube runs over the edge of the trough, masked by ivy, to a low-output submersible pump. The pump cable ducted out of the trough is also masked by the ivy and connected to an outside electricity supply via a current breaker, which is essential for safety. Apart from occasional topping up the trough with water, this feature requires little or no maintenance. In very cold areas where freezing could be a problem, it may be necessary for this type of water feature to be drained in winter and the pump dry stored.

The glazed trough water feature has duckweed floating on the surface and *Soleirolia soleirolii* at the base.

Hornbeam arch

There are two gates into the garden, both framed with an arch. The traditional oak gate has a hornbeam, *Carpinus betulus*, screen-trained over it to form a dense and lush green arch. These trees have been allowed to grow to 4m (13ft) high, then trained over the path using wire and bamboo canes to provide a dense shelter. They are similar in appearance to beech (*Fagus sylvatica*) with smaller, finer leaves and a fresh light green colour throughout spring and early summer, with the leaves turning butter yellow before falling in autumn. Hornbeam tends to tolerate heavier, wetter soils than beech and is ideal for this heavy clay ground.

SECLUDED INTIMATE GARDEN

PLANTS and PLANTING

Even in small gardens, trees and large shrubs are necessary to create the feeling of enclosure and a cosy atmosphere. This garden has several small- to medium-sized trees that provide interest at different times of the year. Positioned in the centre is a *Prunus subhirtella* 'Autumnalis', which as its name suggests is the autumn flowering cherry tree. However, it also flowers intermittently through the winter and early spring with small white flowers on bare stems. It provides a light canopy in summer that allows plenty of underplanting, including a *Photinia* 'Palette', which provides winter evergreen structure, surrounded by a carpet of *Geranium* x *cantabrigiense* 'Cambridge' with pale pink flowers.

Many slightly tender plants are to be found in this garden as it is in a sheltered position on a gentle slope. However, the soil is a clay loam over heavy yellow clay and poor drainage caused problems when establishing the yew hedge (see page 138 to learn how this has been overcome). The pH is slightly acid and large quantities of sharp washed sand and mushroom compost have been incorporated.

The key positions for structural planting are filled with evergreen shrubs including *Hebe salicifolia*, *Buxus sempervirens* 'Marginata' and *Pittosporum tenuifolium*. *Rosa* 'Leontine Gervais' scrambles over the pergolas with *Clematis* 'Mme Baron Veillard' and *Clematis viticella* 'Julia Correvon' framing the view down the pathway.

Catalpa x *erubescens* 'Purpurea' with pink and purple underplanting creates tonal harmony.

Buxus sempervirens 'Marginata' provides an evergreen structure surrounded by the apricot *Geum* 'Leonard's Variety'. *Euphorbia wulfenii* (above left) makes a good contrast in foliage.

Catalpa x *erubescens* 'Purpurea' (zone 5), the heavier canopy of the purple form of Indian bean tree, can be controlled by hard pruning if necessary, though the harder it is pruned the stronger it seems to grow. Thriving in this sheltered positioned protected by the hornbeam hedge, it has small white snapdragon-like flowers that are spotted with pink above the dark purple, almost black, new growths. It will, if left unpruned, reach up to 10x10m (33x33ft). It is normally the last tree to burst into leaf in late spring, possibly even as late as early summer. The canopy can provide excellent shade during summer due to very large rounded leaves. Once established, after a year or two, growth becomes very rapid. Plant in fertile, well-drained soil.

Buxus sempervirens 'Marginata' (zones 5–6) is a slow-growing variegated box that provides evergreen structure. It should be clipped once a year, during late spring or early summer after the danger of late frost has passed. As a fussy foliage plant it needs toning down and planting in combination with plain green leaves. Here it is surrounded by **Geum 'Leonard's Variety'** (zone 4), which has rounded light green leaves and bright apricot/pink flowers that tone in well with the creamy yellow variegation in summer. Plant in drifts for best effect and trim back lightly after flowering to encourage a later flush of flower. It is an excellent 'edge of border' plant, growing to 20cm (8in) high. Equally useful and even lower growing is the white-flowered *Geum rivale* 'Album'.

The shiny green seedheads of *Lotus hirsutum* gradually change to rich ruby red.

Hebe salicifolia provides evergreen structure and many months of flowering.

The glossy heart-shaped green leaves of *Clerodendron bungei* can be seen in the foreground with *Nepita govaniana* behind.

Lotus hirsutum (zones 7–10), formerly known as *Dorycnium hirsutum, is* named for the hirsute (hairy) foliage. The attractive soft-textured grey leaves form a mound up to 1m (3ft) high and 1.2m (4ft) across. The white pea flowers are flushed with pink and appear during early to midsummer and by late summer shiny green fruits form that gradually turn dark reddish brown into autumn. It is a very low-maintenance shrub that tolerates drought but requires well-drained soil and a sunny aspect. Trim this shrub in late spring to retain a bushy habit. One of my favourite shrubs, it is a very versatile plant and can be used in many different planting combinations.

Hebe salicifolia (zones 5–9) is a white-flowered evergreen shrub growing to about 2.4x2.4m (8x8ft) if left unchecked. I prefer to prune it every two or three years to maintain a bushy plant of about 1.5x1.5m (5x5ft). Pruning should be carried out soon after flowering. The problem is that in milder areas I have known this plant to continue to flower all year and then the safest time to prune hard is during early summer. This may delay flowering by a few weeks but is worth it to ensure that there are plenty of fresh shoots. An alternative is to prune in two stages. First remove about half the tallest branches in early summer and, when there is an abundance of new growth from the base, remove the rest of the old branches in midsummer.

Clerodendron bungei (zones 5–11) is a slightly tender suckering shrub that grows up to 3m (10ft) high with heart-shaped leaves and corymbs of deep rose-coloured flowers in late summer. The leaves are purplish green in colour with an unpleasant smell and the stems are dark green with a darker mottling. Once established it is difficult to remove and sends suckers in all directions including, in this garden, through the informal brick path. This is not a problem if they are removed during the first growing season. However, if left for longer, they are anchored by a deep tap root that requires considerable effort to dig out. Nevertheless, this is still well worth growing for late summer colour.

The woolly silver leaves of *Stachys lanata* provide a good foil for the very dark purple heads of *Lavandula* 'Helmsdale'.

Lavandula 'Helmsdale' is planted in a dense group to maximize the impact of its highly scented foliage.

The oak pergola is clothed by the apricot flowers of rambling *Rosa* 'Leontine Gervais'.

Stachys lanata (zones 4–8) has very silver leaves due to a covering of a mass of fine hairs. These help to conserve water and thus this plant can survive in arid conditions. Heavy, wet soils are not ideal for stachys and in this garden it is planted close to the edge of the path on a slight slope in the hope that it will overwinter successfully. It is a useful plant when used repetitively along a narrow border or pathway to provide 'pools' of silver in between taller planting. *Stachys byzantina* 'Silver Carpet' is the non-flowering, low-growing form.

Lavandula 'Helmsdale' (zone 8) requires free-draining soil conditions and plenty of sun. It is a cultivar of French lavender, *Lavandula stoechas*, that flowers from early summer for up to six weeks and then benefits from a gentle trim before putting on more growth and flowering again during late summer. This cultivar varies from the type, which has pale pink flowerheads, in that it has very dark purple and red bracts and flowers that are almost black. As with all lavenders, it is relatively short lived, surviving perhaps six or seven years in free-draining soils and less in heavier ground. Indeed it may even require replacing every year which in many cases is worth it as the unusual dark flower colour, combined with highly scented foliage, is difficult to substitute with another variety.

Rosa 'Leontine Gervais' (zones 4–8) is a vigorous variety ideal for pergola or trellis. Do not attempt to grow it on a wall or solid fence as it will suffer from mildew and black spot. Its sprawling habit makes it a good choice for any framework or for threading through a tree. Almost all ramblers flower only once during the season. However, they last for up to six weeks or more and provide a mass of flowers all at once. This variety also has the advantage of glossy leaves with reddish leaf stalks that provide good cover as well as a perfect foil for the apricot-pink flowers. To extend the season with a longer show of flowers, you can plant it with later flowering *Clematis* 'Mme Baron Veillard' and *Clematis viticella* 'Julia Correvon'.

The deep pink flowers of *Chelone obliqua* contrast with the dark green leaves. The tight green buds ensure a succession of flowers during late summer.

The bold green leaves of *Hydrangea aspera sargentiana* contrast well against the silvery leaves of *Pittosporum* 'Silver Queen'.

A hedge of *Carpinus betulus* (hornbeam) arches over the front gate, creating natural privacy and an intriguing sense of mystery.

Chelone obliqua (zones 3–9), commonly known as turtlehead, is a herbaceous perennial that reaches 60–90cm (2–3ft) by the time it flowers in late summer. The leaves are rounded, dark green and toothed with deep rose-pink flowers that form in clusters at the top of each stem. The plant quickly forms a dense clump and is easily propagated by division during early spring. It thrives in moist, rich soil in either full sun or partial shade but is prone to mildew if grown in dry conditions. There is also a white variety, *Chelone obliqua* 'Alba', but this has a weaker constitution and paler green leaves.

Hydrangea aspera sargentiana (zones 5–9) will grow to 2.4m (8ft) high and 1.8m (6ft) wide and in this garden will probably outgrow its present position. However, by the time it reaches full size a number of the infill underplanting varieties will have died out anyway, allowing the hydrangea the space it deserves. It is a useful late summer flowering plant requiring some shelter but otherwise quite hardy. I have known this plant to be frosted each year as the first new shoots of spring appear. But it soon recovers and develops bristly dark green leaves followed by large heads of pink and purplish blue flowers throughout late summer and autumn. The stems are also attractive with peeling bark. If possible, try to plant a good-sized specimen as it is smaller plants that often fail to establish.

Carpinus betulus (zones 4–8) was used to form the hornbeam arch by simply tying the tops of two young hornbeam trees together when they reached 2.4m (8ft) high. The supple branches were curved gently across the opening and within two growing seasons the arch was formed. Trimming the hedge is best carried out during late summer. This is normal practice for most hedges as they should then put on a small amount of growth that will ripen before winter and yet remain tidy for the rest of the year. For small-leaved hedging plants, a pair of shears or a hedge trimmer is fine but, with large leaves such as laurel or rhododendron hedges, the shoots should be individually pruned or the result can be an unsightly and untidy wall of cut and chewed foliage.

There are many reasons for success or failure in establishing a garden and so often, if a plant fails to thrive, it is due to a combination of conditions rather than one single reason.

Climate and soil conditions

Unless we are growing in protected environments, such as greenhouses and polytunnels, there is little we can do about the climate and it is therefore important to understand, in broad terms, the conditions we are likely to encounter through the various seasons. Much of this has to be learned through trial and error but hopefully the following pages will help to reduce the 'error' factor.

There has always been a fairly clear definition of hardy, half-hardy and tender plants, but many of us are tempted to push the boundaries by growing varieties from all over the world that originate from extreme climates and expecting them to thrive in alien conditions. It is very important to ensure that the framework of your garden, such as hedges, trees and all the structural planting, should be of the type able to thrive in your climate. By all means take some risks with your planting but not with structural elements of the garden. You could, for example, plant *Ilex crenata* for a tough small evergreen hedge rather than rely on a plant such as rosemary, because a whole hedge of rosemary can be spoiled even if only one or two plants suffer. You can easily replace the odd rosemary if it fails when used within borders, but a hedge is ruined by the gaps and varying sizes of plants.

One very simple way to get an idea of what will survive best in your garden is to look around at the vegetation that naturally grows in the area and in other gardens.

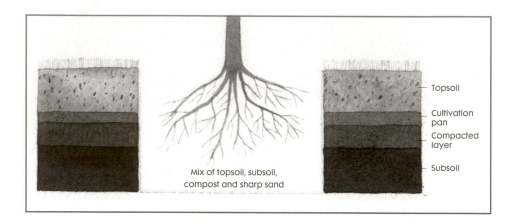

Mix of topsoil, subsoil, compost and sharp sand

Topsoil

Cultivation pan

Compacted layer

Subsoil

Typical profile of heavy clay soils, showing cultivation pan and compacted layer.

Willows, birch trees and sedges will indicate wet areas, while elder, yew, thorn and beech are a fair guide to well-drained land. The presence of rhododendrons, azaleas, camellias and pieris are an indication that the soil is of an acid type – that is, free of lime.

However, before planting anything in your garden I strongly advise you to learn a little about the soil conditions. To do this, first of all dig a hole at least 60cm (2ft) and if possible 90cm (3ft) deep and study the soil profile.

Heavy soils

Heavy clay soils are considered often to be the most difficult, but at least they hold on to nutrients and can be improved. The main problems are waterlogging in the winter and cracking up due to drying out in the summer. Mulching twice a year in late winter and early summer with plenty of organic matter, such as mushroom compost or leaf mould, will help retain moisture in summer and make the soil easier to work. Over time, worms will take the mulch down into the topsoil. Incorporating sharp grit will also break up heavy clay soil but will not necessarily solve drainage problems. It

is often thought that on poorly drained soils larger holes need to be dug out with drainage material put at the bottom. This does not, in fact, solve a drainage problem, it will simply act as a sump as the water has no means of escape. In this case drainage needs to be put in to carry the water away from the planting site or you will have to choose plants that will tolerate waterlogging in winter.

Another problem on heavy soils, in particular, is compaction. This can be either surface compaction or a hard pan created by compaction from several centimetres up to 50cm (20in) or so below the surface.

Surface compaction, or capping, is less of a problem to overcome. The main cause of this is over-cultivation, which breaks down the soil texture into very fine a particles that when wet form a porridge-like consistency with no air pockets. This then dries out to become more like concrete than good garden soil. Regular mulching and incorporation of organic matter, mushroom or garden compost, will help in these circumstances, as will the incorporation of grit or sharp sand.

The causes of sub-surface compaction are often mechanical – caused by either regular ploughing or rotavating to the same depth or, as often found on new developments, the ground has been compacted by construction machinery and a layer of topsoil has been placed on top, causing major problems later. This will be discovered when digging your soil profile pit and it is vital that compaction should be eased before planting, by either deep digging or using a mechanical digger or sub-soiler.

On heavy soils damage can be caused by cultivation and walking on the ground in wet conditions. Try to keep off the garden when the ground is wet, but if it is absolutely necessary, then I suggest working from a sheet of plywood, laid on the ground to avoid compaction of the soil.

Roses are particularly good on heavy soils provided the drainage is adequate. Silver-leafed plants such as lavender and artemisia, however, are less easy to grow on heavy soils.

Light soils

Although the antithesis of heavy clay, similar treatment – the incorporation of organic matter such as mushroom or organic compost – is needed for light soils because the main problem is normally lack of moisture retention. Because water runs through light sandy soils very easily, nutrients are also leached out quite quickly so your plants will need more food as well as water. The advantage of light soils is that there is little likelihood of compaction and they can be cultivated in most weather conditions. They also warm up early in the year, encouraging early growth in your plants. In the past peat has been used to increase the moisture retention in light soils but I would avoid the use of peat for soil conditioning as it is a non-renewable resource. There are plenty of other alternatives for soil conditioning, including garden compost, composted bark and mushroom compost. It is best to find a compost that is readily available in your area and cheap enough to be used liberally.

SOIL TIPS

● In dry weather light hoeing of the surface to form a fine tilth about 1cm (½in) thick will act as a mulch, reducing moisture loss during the summer as well as getting rid of weed seedlings.

● It is common practice on poor soils, whether they are heavy or light, to bring in good quality topsoil. Wherever possible I recommend that existing soil should be improved rather than replaced.

● For soil improvement and mulching it is best to use decomposed material such as well-rotted manure, mushroom compost or well-rotted garden compost because these feed the ground as well as improve the structure. If you apply wood chip, straw, wood shavings or other partially rotted organic matter, the rotting process will use up nitrogen in the soil, reducing the levels available for your plants. Therefore, it is necessary to top up with high-nitrogen fertilizer.

● If mulching to retain moisture during dry periods, always soak the ground thoroughly before applying the mulch.

● If the garden is drying out and you have to choose what to water first, give priority to evergreen shrubs. The deciduous plants can always lose some leaves prematurely and recover later. Evergreens will suffer more lasting damage.

Mediterranean plants, such as rosemary, lavender, salvia and cistus thrive on light, well-drained soils. If you must grow roses in light sandy conditions, then a species rose will do better than the hybrids. *Rosa virginiana* and *Rosa nitida* are particularly good and disease free with simple single pink flowers, good hips and excellent autumn colour.

Lawns and other turf areas

Grasses have surprisingly deep roots and it is often possible to gain some idea of the soil conditions by looking carefully at a well-established lawn, particularly during dry periods when traces of buried rubble, old walls, paving or tree stumps become apparent from above. Soil compaction is also easily identified and, rather than simply dealing with the symptoms of a poorly drained lawn by killing the moss, it is often better to deal with the cause by easing the compaction, or in some way introducing air to the ground, either by use

of a lawn spiker, garden fork or coring tool. Afterwards rake in sharp sand as both air and water are required at the roots.

In some circumstances it may be necessary to install drainage as well as ease the compaction. Ideally this should be carried out during dry conditions to avoid causing damage to the soil structure. As my local drainage contractor says: 'View when it is wet, do when it is dry.'

Creating the right conditions for your plants

It is often better to work with the existing conditions rather than attempt to alter them, although it is possible to improve extremes in soil quality as already described. However, to cope with varying extremes such as dry shade, moist shade, dry sunny aspects, moist sunny aspects, shallow thin soils or deep rich soils, a careful choice of plants is essential to avoid a struggle with nature.

For lists of plants for specific sites I find a good reference is *The Hillier Manual of Trees and Shrubs* (see page 144), which at the back has headings for various conditions and lists plants that are suitable for each one.

Ground conditions affect the type of growth in any plant and often determine the degree of extreme weather that can be withstood. For example, lavenders and other silver-leafed plants that have very fine hairs on the stems and leaves, which give them the silver appearance, can be severely damaged or killed outright by low temperatures when grown in heavier poorly drained ground. In well-drained soils, however, it seems they are able to withstand lower temperatures more easily. Therefore, if you are having problems with growing plants that have borderline hardiness in your area and the ground is prone to staying wet during winter, improving the drainage or openness of the ground may increase the chances of their survival.

The condition of a plant at the time adverse conditions occur will also have a bearing on its ability to survive. Soft sappy growth on woody plants, in particular, is prone to damage by low temperatures and cold winds, so as autumn approaches reduce feeding and avoid doses of high-nitrogen feed towards the end of summer. Regular feeding should start late spring until midsummer.

Autumn, winter or spring planting?

This is a question regularly asked and as usual there is no plain and simple answer. The tradition of only autumn/winter planting originates from the days before garden centres when nurseries supplied plants dug up during the dormant season. Then we had little choice but to plant at this time. Since the 1960s when pot-grown trees, shrubs and perennials became available we have been able to plant at virtually any time of year,

provided the ground is not frozen. Planting during a heat wave or during drought is also not to be recommended.

Location as well as soil condition plays a large part in determining when to plant. On light soils, in any location, autumn planting is fine for most varieties other than the most tender subjects. On heavier soils, especially in exposed conditions, it may be better to plant in spring. A plant put in the ground in autumn just as it becomes dormant may sit in cold, wet conditions for four to five months, leaving the roots prone to rotting during that time, whereas if it is planted in spring it should start growing as soon as the soil is firmed around its rootball. A disadvantage of spring planting is that early periods of drought can subject young plants to a lack of water, and you need to be extra vigilant to see that enough water is available to get the plants established.

As a general rule I favour autumn planting for hardy trees and shrubs, including roses, on all soils other than extremely wet, and spring to early summer planting of the more tender and rot-prone subjects, such as lavender, nepeta, achillea, rosemary, salvia and dicentra. With careful watering during early summer,

An example of a bare-rooted bush rose showing a long hypercotyl between stem and root.

container-grown shrubs and perennials planted in late spring often overtake those planted the previous autumn. Bare-rooted and rootballed plants must still be planted during late autumn and spring, in ground that is frost free and not too wet.

Roses supplied bare rooted are good subjects for winter planting provided the roots are carefully pruned.

Planting depth

The correct planting depth is critical to the survival and success of all plants. Usual good advice is to plant to the same depth that the tree or shrub has been grown at before or that the plant has been in the pot. Planting too deep is in my view one of the three main causes of failure to establish new plants (the other two are drying out and waterlogging). Some plants are more susceptible to this problem than others and it is more crucial in heavy, poorly drained soils than in lighter, well-drained ground. Japanese maples, apple trees, birch and mountain ash are but a few that I have seen suffer in this way. If planted too deep, the bark will slowly rot away during winter, only to recover slightly during the following growing season, and again deteriorate the following year, particularly in heavy ground. At best the tree will survive but hang on by a thread; at worst it will die after the first winter. Japanese maples are particularly prone to this as the bark is very thin. As always there are exceptions and some woody plants readily root from their stems if buried. These include forsythia, poplar, willow and dogwood.

Another exception is clematis, which should be planted 5–10cm (2–4in) deeper than in the pot. The aim is to keep the roots cool to avoid the disease clematis wilt. Planting a small shrub to shade the clematis roots will also help keep them cool.

Roses have a particularly deep root on young plants. When supplied they will either

A bush rose, pruned and planted with the hypercotyl, covered by at least 4cm (1½in) of soil and mulch.

be bare rooted or containerized. If sold in a container, the roots will have been pruned, partly to encourage more fibre and also to fit the plant into a pot. Although rose pots are deeper than normal, they are often still too shallow to pot up the rose to the required depth, and the section between root and stem called the hypercotyl is left exposed. It is important that this hypercotyl be covered by at least 4cm (1½in) for the plant to thrive. This is because the variety you buy starts life as a tiny bud, taken from the parent plant and inserted into the hypercotyl of a root stock closely related to the wild rose. This budding or graft should be kept moist and below the surface. Unfortunately, in my experience, it is a common sight to see roses either supplied in pots or planted in gardens high out of the ground. In the case of well-established plants,

do not dig them up in order to lower them. Instead, simply put a thick layer of mulch around the base.

Pruning

Pruning is a subject that worries many gardeners, who are afraid of pruning too hard, at the wrong time or not hard enough. There are two main ways of pruning – trimming and thinning. Trimming is normally carried out on hedges and individual shrubs to keep them to a definite formal shape. These include box, myrtle, pittosporum, yew, holly, lavender and rosemary. Thinning is done to retain a more natural shape of plant and is often referred to as replacement pruning. This is the removal of older wood when flowers have finished to allow for the regeneration of growth from lower down the plant. Plants that require this type of pruning and are often neglected or pruned incorrectly are late spring and early

summer flowering shrubs such as forsythia, philadelphus, spiraea, deutzia, weigela and shrub roses that flower only once.

The principle of replacement pruning is first to remove dead and diseased wood. Any pruning should start with this. Then remove all the stems that have had flowers on them down to a few centimetres above the base. It should be obvious which are new shoots.

Having dispensed with the older wood, this ensures that the new growth during the remaining growing season will develop and produce plenty of flowers next year. A plant that has been pruned should still be able to look attractive and not unsightly. Shaping a tree or shrub is also an important aspect of pruning. Plants flower more profusely from the horizontal branches than vertical and this

Use hardy plants such as box for structural planting and, when watering, give them priority over deciduous plants until well established.

Philadelphus 'Manteau d'Hermine' in midsummer just after flowering is over (above). Remove older recently flowered stems to within 4–8cm (1½–3in) of their base (below), leaving the shorter new shoots complete to flower the following spring or early summer (right).

should be borne in mind when pruning roses, climbers and fruit trees. A number of perennial hardy plants such as hardy geraniums, *Salvia nemerosa* varieties, alchemilla and nepeta can be cut almost to the ground after their first flush of flowers (normally midsummer), which will encourage them to put on more new growth and produce a second flush of flowers later in the summer.

Almost all plants respond very well to pruning and indeed a general rule is the harder the pruning the more vigorous the regrowth. However, some shrubs and trees should only have minor pruning and, only when necessary, should complete limbs or branches be removed to avoid unsightly stubby ends of branches. These include magnolias, acers and hamamelis. Rhododendrons should only be pruned when they become too large but you may lose one season's flowering as the flower buds are formed in early summer. They normally regenerate quite well but will look unsightly for a time if pruned very hard.

Euphorbias, such as *Euphorbia wulfenii*, must have their flowered stems removed by the early summer as they become unsightly.

The lime-green heads of *Euphorbia wulfenii* have faded by early summer (above). Remove old stems to within 4–8cm (1½–3in) of their base (below), leaving the shorter new shoots complete to flower the following spring (right).

Cut as low as possible to allow the new growth, which should by then be growing quite vigorously, to thrive in readiness for the following spring's flowering. Care should be taken with euphorbias as the sap can cause skin and eye irritation. Do not work with them in bright sunlight and always wear gardening gloves and long sleeves.

When deadheading perpetual-flowering roses, do not simply nip off the rose head but try to remove the flower stalk as if you are cutting the rose for putting in a vase. This is a form of summer pruning that will encourage more vigorous growth and flowering.

Watering and feeding

Lack of water during the first few days and weeks of planting is, in my view, the most common reason for failure, although planting of rot-prone plants in heavy soils during autumn comes a close second. Most container-grown plants are grown in a peat-based compost that, once dried out, absorbs water more slowly than the surrounding soil. It is, therefore, essential to ensure that the rootball of a plant is thoroughly wet before planting. This does not mean soaking for hours at a time. Before planting simply dunk the rootball in a bucket of water for a few minutes until the bubbles stop, remembering that until the roots have begun to grow out from the original pot shape into the garden soil the plant is acting rather like a wick drawing moisture only from the original ball of root. For spring or early summer planting in particular, it is essential that water is frequently applied at the base of each plant. Once they have been established for a growing season, general overhead or low-level watering will be sufficient during dry periods. As a general rule during dry periods it is far better to soak your plants thoroughly once a week or fortnight rather than regular fine sprinkling every day, which never reaches far below the surface. Deciduous shrubs and perennials helpfully

Mix of topsoil, subsoil and grit

Topsoil

Subsoil

Shingle

Drainage pipe

Soil profile showing drainage and soil improvement for yew hedge.

show signs of lack of water immediately and should perk up soon after they have been soaked. However, evergreens may not show any sign for some weeks, by which time it can be too late. A few yellow leaves throughout an evergreen plant such as an eleagnus or myrtle in summer is a sure sign that perhaps a few weeks earlier they were allowed to dry out. Drying out causes a great deal of stress to a plant, especially those not adapted for extreme conditions of drought. For example, roses and honeysuckle may quickly develop mildew if allowed to become too dry.

The more watering that is carried out, the more feed will be required to top up the goodness leached out by watering. This is more important on light, open soils than on heavy clay loams. Compost mulching should be sufficient but on hungry soils it may be necessary to top this up using blood, fish and bone or similar. Do not overfeed as this can have the same effect as shortage of water. Also remember that too much soft growth late in summer leaves plants prone to frost damage. With some plants too much growth will also reduce the amount of flower.

Unfortunately the symptoms of lack of water are often the same as those for too much water and both result in root death and affect the foliage above. The ever-popular

yew hedging is difficult to establish on heavy wet soils and good drainage is essential to ensure success. The problem in establishing a yew hedge on poorly drained soil is that the lower part of the rootball will rot during wet winter periods and the plant will take on a very bronzed appearance by spring. At worst the plant will die by early summer. At best it may struggle to grow through it. However, a common scenario is that new roots develop in spring near the surface that are just enough to keep the plant alive although rather sick looking. During the summer these roots close to the surface dry out and the plant is continually under stress, before eventually dying and several years may have been lost in establishing your yew hedge.

Profuse flowering is not always a sign of a healthy plant and there are circumstances when a plant has flowered better than ever before and then died. This is a natural process whereby the plant, whether it be a garden or pot plant, is under threat for one reason or another and flowers in a desperate effort to reproduce before it dies. There are, however, some varieties that are naturally short lived and flower very profusely during a short period. For example, *Erysimum* 'Bowles' Mauve' (perennial wallflower) flowers for a few months with masses of flower, but may only live for three or four years. Cytisus (brooms) are very similar and normally only live for eight or nine years. These cannot be transplanted easily and special care should be taken when digging close by the roots of established cytisus plants.

Staking and tying

Some of the traditional perennial plants such as delphiniums and peonies may require high maintenance, including the support of careful staking to ensure success. This is fine if you have time. However, I tend to avoid staking perennials wherever possible and use link stakes or hazel twigs when absolutely necessary for tall-growing such as geraniums, salvias and physostegia. Wherever possible it is preferable to plant in such a way that the groupings work as a team to support each other. A good example of this is *Thalictrum aquilegiifolium,* which always requires some support. If planted at the base of a large shrub rose, the branches of the rose should act as support and look good at the same time.

Standard and feathered trees should always be staked. Indeed, large shrubs should also be secured to avoid the roots rocking during the early stages of establishment. Low-level staking is preferable and less unsightly.

I prefer to use galvanized wire and vine eyes to support plants growing up walls. This system works with most structures although it can be difficult on flint walls. Wires should be approximately 45cm (18in) apart running horizontally, starting at least 20cm (8in) from a corner, window or doorway. Wires should be threaded through vine eyes and be approximately 2cm (1in) from the wall. Once the galvanized wire has oxidized, it is hardly visible and the plants can be attached with soft string as they grow.

Climbing roses may be grown on a wall but ramblers should always be grown on open structures such as pergolas and trellises, allowing a free flow of air through the branches; otherwise, they are susceptible to mildew. Consider growing clematis particularly through roses with *a* single flowering period to increase the season of interest. Plant a rose on the sunny side of the pergola with the clematis roots on the shaded side.

Above **Grow rambling roses on open structures to allow free movement of air through the branches.**

Left **Tie in shoots of climbing plants like *Solanum jasminoides* 'Album' to galvanized wires secured with vine eyes.**

SOURCES

Places to visit
See the National Gardens Scheme 'Yellow Book' for over 3000 gardens in England and Wales to visit, including my own garden at Leydens, Stick Hill, Edenbridge, Kent.

For more ideas visit these traditional gardens; three among many that have provided me with ideas and enthsiasm for traditional design and plantings.

Hever Castle Gardens
Hever
Edenbridge
Kent TN8
www.hever-castle.co.uk

Hidcote Manor Garden
Hidcote Bartrim, Nr
Chipping Campden
Gloucestershire GL55 6LR
www.nationaltrust.org.uk

Tissinghurst Castle Gardens
Sissinghurst
Nr. Cranbrook TN17 2AB
www.nationaltrust.org.uk/places/sissinghurst/

Useful references
The R.H.S. Plantfinder, Royal Horticultural Society/Dorling Kindersley, updated annually

The Hillier Manual of Trees and Shrubs, David & Charles 1994

The R.H.S. Encyclopedia of Plants & Flowers, Dorling Kindersley 1989

Hardy Herbaceous Perennials, Vols. 1 & 2, Leo Jelitto & Wilhelm Schacht, Batsford 1990

Making the Most of Clematis, Raymond J. Evison, Burrall Floraprint 1987

Trees for Your Garden, Roy Lancaster, Burall Floraprint 1974

Roses, Roger Phillips and Martyn Rix, Pan Books Ltd 1988

Useful Contacts
The Royal Horticultural Society
80 Vincent Square
London SW1P 2PE
www.rhs.org.uk

The National Gardens Scheme
Hatchlands Park
East Clandon
Guildford
Surrey GU4 7RT
www.ngs.org.uk

Garden Design
Roger Platts Garden Design & Nurseries
Stick Hill
Edenbridge
Kent TN8 5NH
www.rogerplatts.co.uk

Paving materials
B.S. Eaton
Coppice Lane
Cheslyn Hay
WALSALL
WS6 7EY
www.bseaton.co.uk

Bricks
Freshfield Lane Brickworks
Danehill
Haywards Heath
West Sussex RH17 7HH
www.flb.uk.com

Garden Lighting
Spruce Lighting
43-45 Quarry Road
Tunbridge Wells
Kent TN1 2EZ

Garden Furniture
Gaze Burvill
Redloh House
2 Michael Road
London SW6 2AD
www.gazeburvill.com

Walkham Teak Ltd
Holewell Farm
Walkhampton
Yelverton
Devon PL20 6LW
www.walkham.co.uk

Garden Ornament
Bulbeck Foundry
Reach Road
Burwell
Cambridgeshire
CB5 0AH
www.bulbeckfoundry.co.uk

Pots and Pithoi
The Barns
East Street
Turners Hill
West Sussex
RH10 4QQ
www.pots-and-pithoi.co.uk

Room in the Garden
Oak Cottage
Furzen Lane
Ellens Green
Rudgewick
West Sussex RH12 3AR
www.roominthegarden.co.uk

Plants
Roger Platts Nurseries
Stick Hill
Edenbridge
Kent TN8 5NH
www.rogerplatts.co.uk

Jekka's Herb Farm
Rose Cottage
Shellards Lane
Alveston
Bristol BS35 3SY
www.jekkasherbfarm.com

David Austin Roses Ltd
Bowling Green Lane
Albrighton
Wolverhampton WV7 3HB
www.davidaustinroses.com

Hardy's Cottage Garden Plants
Priory Lane Nursery
Freefolk Priors
Whitchurch
Hants RG28 7NJ
www.hardys-plants.co.uk

W. E. Th. Ingwersen Ltd
Birch Farm Nursery
Gravetye
East Grinstead
West Sussex RH19 4LE
www.ingwersen.co.uk

Pottery
Whichford Pottery
Whichford
Shipston-on-Stour
Warwickshire CV36 5PG
www.whichfordpottery.com

Reclaimed building materials
Ajeer Ltd
Sugar Loaf Yard
Brightling Road
Woods Corner
Nr Heathfield
East Sussex TN21 9LL

Solopark
Station Road
Nr Pampisford
Cambridgeshire CB2 4HB
01223 834663
www.solopark.co.uk

Pergolas, Buildings and Greenhouses
Roger Platts Oak Pergolas and Summerhouses
Stick Hill
Edenbridge
Kent TN8 5NH
www.rogerplatts.co.uk

C. H Whitehouse Ltd
Buckhurst Works
Bells Yew Green
Tunbridge Wells
Kent TN39 BN

The Children's Cottage Company
The Sanctuary
Shobrook
Crediton
Devon EX17 1BG
www.play-houses.com

Miscellaneous
English Hurdle
Curload
Stoke St. Gregory
Taunton
Somerset TA3 6JD
www.hurdle.co.uk

Felco secateurs
Felco/Burton Mcall Ltd
163 Parker Drive
Leicester LE4 0JP
www.burton-mccall.co.uk

INDEX

Page numbers in *italic* indicate entries with illustrations.

ACKNOWLEDGEMENTS

With thanks to all those who have
helped me in my gardening career
and especially to Jeanette and my
Mother and Father for their
encouragement, love and support.

Thanks are due also to
Colin and Jane Bryan
B.S. Eaton Ltd
Norton and Patricia Goldie-Scot
Ian and Linda King
Dennis and Jackie Mahoney
Neil and Jackie Walker

Mavis Sweetingham
Nick Jupp
Jane Streatfeild
Adam Bradstock
Helen Greenfield
Daniel Newberry
The National Gardens Scheme
The Royal Horticultural Society
Pippa Rubinstein and
Judith Robertson
Steven Wooster
Nicky Cooney